EASY SHMEEZY
GUIDE TO
HEBREW

R' MOSHE SHERIZEN

MENUCHA
PUBLISHERS

A PROJECT OF THE

Easy-Shmeezy
Foundation

THE EASY-SHMEEZY GUIDE TO HEBREW

R' MOSHE SHERIZEN

Copyright 2014 by Moshe Sherizen

Second Edition February 2015

ISBN: 978-1-61465-066-9

בספר זה אין שום חשש גניזה ומותר לקראו בכל חדרי הבית
וכמו כן מותר ללמוד ממנו בליל ניט"ל.

Executive Producer: Rabbi Shmuel Elbinger

Book Design: Rivkah Lewis

Published and distributed by
Menucha Publishers Inc.
250 44th street
Brooklyn N.Y. 11232
Tel/Fax: 718-232-0856
1-855-Menucha
Sales@Menuchapublishers.com
www.Menuchapublishers.com

For inquiries regarding The Easy-Shmeezy Guide to
Hebrew, or to find out more about learning Hebrew
check out www.EasyShmeezy.com

In loving memory of my dear father

Eliezer Avraham Tzvi
ben Pesachya Leib Sherizen

נלב״ע י״ז מנחם אב תשע״ד

Abba loved learning Torah and living Torah.
He taught me dedication to family,
community and Eretz Yisrael.

The sterling example he set for his
children and grandchildren will endure
for generations to come.

**Interested in some awesome mp3s
that go along with this book?**
Go to www. EasyShmeezy.com to download
mp3 lessons that walk you through the book,
every step of the way. In no time at all you'll be
speakin' Hebrew like a real *sabra*.

For any questions or comments regarding this
book, or to get involved in the publication of
future Easy-Shmeezy guides, visit us at:

www.EasyShmeezy.com

All mistakes found in this book are purely
intentional and they are my way of
keeping your atenttion.

TABLE OF CONTENTS

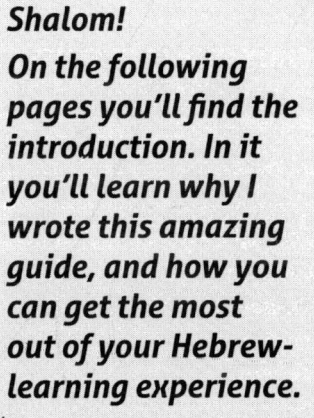

Shalom!
On the following pages you'll find the introduction. In it you'll learn why I wrote this amazing guide, and how you can get the most out of your Hebrew-learning experience.

Sent April 15, 2013
From: ShwartzFam33@gmail.com
To: Msherizen@gmail.com

Hi Moshe,

Thanks for your easy-shmeezy Yiddish book, it really is fun for the whole family. Each week at the Shabbos table we take it out and learn a *bisl* Yiddish together. We also really enjoy the humor element of the book. Sometimes when I read the Easy-Shmeezy it's so entertaining that I don't even realize that I'm learning new words. I was wondering if you'd be so kind to bless the public with the same kind of book to teach Hebrew. You see, I've been living in Israel now for 5 years but I never really got the hang of Hebrew. Israelis talk so fast, and whenever I try speaking Hebrew, after my first sentence they usually say "You kan speek wiss me in Eenglish, I anderstand you better."

What I really liked about your style is that you divide the language up into different sections, making it very user-friendly. I believe that if I had an Easy-Shmeezy Hebrew Guide it would enable me to speak with confidence and pride. Besides people living in Israel there are so many *Yehu-dim* (Jews) all over the world who use Hebrew on a daily basis in prayer and Torah study. Many of them aren't really familiar with the translation and meaning of what they are saying. There are also so many Jews coming close to *Yahadut* (Judaism) later on in life and it's especially difficult for them get into the Hebrew part of the religion. Even just reading Hebrew is tricky for the newcomer! If they'd have your easy-shmeezy format I think they'd feel more comfortable and less intimidated by the new language.

Once again, thank you Moshe, and please be in touch if I can be of any assistance. And just to get you started, later today I'll make a little contribution *bli-neder* (I'll try not to forget) to the Easy-Shmeezy Foundation via your website.

Todah Rabbah (Thanks a ton) and keep me posted,

Reuven

p.s. How did you learn Hebrew? And do you teach Hebrew 1 on 1 or know anyone else that does?

Sent April 16 2013
From: Msherizen@gmail.com
To: ShwartzFam33@gmail.com

Greetings Reuven,

Thank you for reaching out to say *shalom*!

It's always nice to hear that people are enjoying the book. It's funny that you mention the Shabbos table idea, because some guy named Yechiel told me that at his *shulchan Shabbat* (Shabbos table) they pick out hard Yiddish words and make a trivia game out of them. I did put a lot of thought into the layout and setup of the various sections in the book, so I'm very happy to hear that you like it.

In regards to Hebrew, I also live in Israel and I know what you mean about having difficulty learning the language. You're not alone my friend! Many people have a hard time learning Hebrew, and even though I speak it fluently, every once in a while I still have an Israeli tell me, "Oh I see you are American — I speak English! You can speak with me in English if you want. Where are you from in America?" (When I answer, "I'm from Detroit," they ask if I know their cousin Yonatan Cohen in Brooklyn. I explain that Brooklyn is 12 hour drive from Detroit, but they just don't get it.)

When I first came to Israel, I had the advantage of having some background in Hebrew....My parents used to speak to each other in Hebrew when they didn't want us kids to understand. When it's bedtime for my kids, I tell my wife "It's time for B-E-D," but my parents used to say "*Od me'at holchim lishon*" (soon they'll go to bed). I always understood more of my parents' Hebrew than I let on, so that's how I had a bit of a foundation to start with.

In addition to that, whenever I'd learn *Chumash* (Torah) with my father *z"l* (ob"m) or mother they'd always make sure that I recognized the *shoresh* (root) of the Hebrew word. And in *shul* my father *z"l* would point to words in the siddur like *harim* (mountains), *sheleg* (snow) and *yamim* (seas); and lift his hands up to the *shamayim* (sky) and show his excitement over the Hebrew language.

Yes, I loved Hebrew, but I was so busy studying Yiddish in my early years here in Israel that my Hebrew wasn't really progressing. It wasn't until around ten years ago that I started to focus on improving my Hebrew at all. Any time I learned a new word, I wrote it down on a pad of paper (writing things down on pads of paper was a very common practice up until the early 2000's). I also tried to speak Hebrew any time I could, even if I didn't say everything properly.

When I got married in 2006 I moved to Neve Yaakov, Jerusalem, which is a very Israeli community. (I know it sounds funny, like duh — of course its Israeli, it's in Israel! But there are many places in Israel with such high concentrations of Anglos that you really don't need to speak more than a few words of Hebrew to get by.) My wife and I lived on a street where we were the only Americans, and we were forced to dive into the Israeli language and culture. I spent many nights hangin' out with my Sefardi *ba'al dira* (landlord) who lived upstairs. We'd drink Turkish coffee and eat *schug* (spicy sauce) and *malawach* (Sefardi pancakes) together. Most importantly, however, he'd always correct my Hebrew mistakes (with a small smirk for good measure).

So that's my Hebrew story in a nutshell. I'm still learning new words all the time; and I actually learned a new word last week, *ledaskes*, which means "to discuss." It's a Hebraized version of the English word "discuss." This is just a small example of the many "Henglish" words that you can hear amongst the modern, hi-tech, Israeli crowd.

You should know, Reuven , that I have been thinking about writing an Easy-Shmeezy Guide to

Hebrew for some time now, and I appreciate your encouragement. I know what you mean about the F.F.Bs who don't really know what they're saying in Hebrew, and also about the B.Ts that find it frustrating to learn a language that's altogether new. The main reason I want to put out a Hebrew book is due to my two passions: 1) Languages, and 2) Helping people...so I hope it will happen soon.

I'll tell you, the reasons I haven't written an Easy-Shmeezy Guide to Hebrew are mainly due to time and money. It takes a ton of work to get any book together, but a language book especially, has many stages that are complicated and time-consuming. It also costs a lot of money to put out such a book, so that's something I have to figure out as well.

Btw, I did receive your generous contribution via PayPal today, and I'm very appreciative. It shows me that people like you really realize the importance of such publications. I'm actually going to sit down this evening and start brainstorming for the book.

I'll keep you posted

Le'hitra'ot (seeya),

Moshe M. Sherizen

P.S. Yes, I do 1-on-1 teaching, but I'm pretty busy with students now and don't have any openings.

But I do work with some excellent teachers who can teach via Skype/phone, so shoot me an email if you'd like some help on that.

• • •

(You can take a 10 second break and breath before you continue reading......breath in.......and out............just like that.)

That email exchange occurred about a year ago. And since then, it's been a busy year at the Easy-Shmeezy Foundation. Putting this book together has really been a labor of love and an amazing adventure. It's also been a great opportunity for me write down some of my thoughts and share some of the humor I find in the Israeli lifestyle.

The book is based on my fool-proof system for learning languages.

It's called the J.E.T System:

J — Jump into the language with confidence: By learning common words and expressions, you'll have the confidence to start integrating into the Hebrew-speaking world. Then you'll have the mindset that you are a Hebrew speaker.

E — Expand your vocabulary: Remember, every word is important. Learn new words to help you become more versatile.

T — Talk, talk, and talk some more: Use your confidence, expressions, and vocab. to speak Hebrew fluently with whoever you can, whenever you can.

If you pick up this book for just a few minutes a day, you'll be surprised to find that within a short period of time you'll be chattin' away like a pro!

Before we start learning Hebrew, I wish to express my appreciation to some very special folks who've helped me along the way.

I am so grateful to my Father z"l and Mother for raising me in the Torah way, and for teaching me to act with sensitivity to those around me. In my parents' home, Eretz Yisrael was always a hot topic. Whether it was the political situation, the *kedusha* (holiness) of the land, or supporting AIPAC and the Technion; Eretz Yisrael was always on their minds. May Hashem bless my mother with *bracha* (blessing), *bri'ut* (health) and *nachat* (naches) from all of her children and grandchildren.

I am so thankful to my dear sister and brother-in-law Naomi and Shlomo Radner. Their support and encouragement have been one of the fundamental ingredients in all of the Easy-Shmeezy productions. This time they topped it off by dedicating this book in memory of our father, Eliezer Avraham Tzvi Sherizen. May the joy that this book brings to others be a *zchus* (merit) for his *neshama* (soul).

I'm also deeply indebted to my teachers and *rebbeim* (Rabbis) past and present. I especially want to thank my Rosh Yeshiva, Rabbi Yehoshua Liff, who has been there to guide me since I got off the plane in Israel twelve years ago; and my Rosh Kollel, Rabbi Aharon Sklar, who taught me how to learn *halacha* (Jewish law) the way Ravina and Rav Ashi would have wanted it done.

The manuscript would not have been ready for print without the assistance of Akiva Beykn and Moshe Tepfer who did an excellent job editing the book; and B. Azar, who did a superb job with the *nikkudot* (vowels). Thanks folks.

At this point I'd also like to recognize the efforts of Rivkah Lewis (lewis.rivkah@gmail.com). Her creative ideas and super-d-duper design really made this book come to life.

Behind every good author stands a good wife. I am deeply indebted to my wife, Batya, who stands behind all of my projects and "great ideas". She inspires me to continue growing and striving to reach greater heights in my *avodas Hashem* (service of G-d). May Hashem grant us the *zchus* of seeing our children continue to grow and live lives of Torah and mitzvos.

Last but certainly not least, I thank Hashem for all of the *chessed* (kindness) that He bestows on me and my family every day. I am especially appreciative that he gave me the opportunity to use my creativity to help others via the Easy-Shmeezies.

I pray that all of *Am Yisrael* (the Jewish nation) will put their differences aside and unite as one and bring *Moshiach* (the Messiah) speedily in our days.

-Moshe Sherizen

BTW in this introduction you've just learned over 20 Hebrew words. Easy-Shmeezy, right?

Transliteration Key

TRANSLITERATION	HEBREW	ENGLISH	AS IN
o	אוֹ	o	hell**o**
a	אַ	ah	p**a**pa
i	אִי	ee	p**i**zza
e	אֶ	e	**e**lephant
ai	אַי	eye	**eye**
ei	אֵי	ei	fr**ei**ght
e	אֱ	e	**e**lephant

Hebrew Alphabet

א	alef	as the "a" in "appropriate"
בּ	bet	as the "b" in "Billy"
ב	vet	as the "v" in "vast"
ג	gimel	as the "g" in game
ד	dalet	as the "d" in door
ה	heh	as the "h" in "hippopotamus"
ו	vav	as the "v" in "vacuum"
ז	zayin	as the "z" in "zoo"
ח	chet	as the "chhh" in the sound of clearing your throat

ט	tet	as the "t" in "tower"
י	yud	as the "y" in "yo-yo"
כ	kaf	as the "k" in "kangaroo"
כ	chaf	as the "chhh" in "Chanukah"
ל	lamed	as the "l" in "limousine"
מ	mem	as the "m" in "Moses"
נ	nun	as the "n" in "nudnik"
ס	samech	as the "s" in "super-d-duper"
ע	ayin	similar to the "alef" but more guttural, most people pronounce it like the alef
פ	peh	as the "p" in "paparazzi"
פ	feh	as the "f" in "falafel"
צ	tzadi	as the "tz" in "tzimmes"
ק	kuf	as the "k" in "koala"
ר	resh	as the "r" in "radical"
שׁ	shin	as the "sh" in "Sherizen"
שׂ	sin	as the "s" in "soul sisters"
ת	tav	as the "t" in "Tel Aviv"

Stress

In Hebrew, stress is usually on the last syllable as in "Tel A**viv**". In words borrowed from other languages, the stress is usually on the first syllable as in "**bar**beque" or "**kug**el."

Gender

In Hebrew, words are defined by gender. The grammar will also change depending on the gender of the subject of the sentence. This is a new concept for many because in English you'd say "I go" for both masculine and feminine whereas in Hebrew, males say *"Ani holech"* and females say *"Ani holechet"*. So in this book I first write the Hebrew expression in the masculine form then I put the feminine form in parentheses. No, it's not because I think women are second class or less important, rather I did it because I wrote the book and I'm a man.

SECTION ONE:
JUMP

Jump in! Take a dive into conversational Hebrew. You're about to learn the most common Hebrew words and expressions. Start using them TODAY. You'll feel like a real sabra.

My First Words
Hamilim Harishonot Sheli
הַמִּלִים הָרִאשׁוֹנוֹת שֶׁלִי

Hi!	Shalom!	שָׁלוֹם!
yes	ken	כֵּן
no	lo	לֹא
please	bevakasha	בְּבַקָשָׁה
Excuse me.	Slicha.	סְלִיחָה.
Thank you.	Toda.	תּוֹדָה.
Oh no!	Oy-va-voy!	אוֹי וַאֲבוֹי
See you later!	Lehitra'ot!	לְהִתְרָאוֹת!

Greetings
Drishat Shalom
דְּרִישַׁת שָׁלוֹם

Hello/Goodbye!	Shalom!	שָׁלוֹם!

How are things?	Ma ha'inyanim?	מָה הָעִנְיָנִים ?
Good morning!	Boker tov!	בֹּקֶר טוֹב !
Good afternoon!	Tzaharayim tovim!	צָהֳרַיִם טוֹבִים !
Good day!	Yom tov!	יוֹם טוֹב !
Good evening!	Erev tov!	עֶרֶב טוֹב !
Good night!	Laila tov!	לַיְלָה טוֹב !
Good week!	Shavu'a tov!	שָׁבוּעַ טוֹב !
Good month!	Chodesh tov!	חֹדֶשׁ טוֹב !
What's up?	Ma nishma?	מַה נִּשְׁמַע ?
What's new?	Ma chadash?	מַה חָדָשׁ ?
What's happening?	Ma koreh?	מַה קוֹרֶה ?
How are you?	Ma shlomcha (shlomech)?	מַה שְׁלוֹמְךָ (שְׁלוֹמֵךְ) ?
Okay.	Beseder.	בְּסֵדֶר.
Fine, thank you.	Tov, toda.	טוֹב, תּוֹדָה.

Thank G-d, great.	Baruch Hashem, metzuyan.	בָּרוּךְ הַשֵּׁם, מְצֻיָּן.
So so.	Kacha kacha.	כָּכָה כָּכָה.
I don't feel well.	Ani lo margish tov (margisha tova).	אֲנִי לֹא מַרְגִּישׁ טוֹב (מַרְגִּישָׁה טוֹבָה).
Have a good trip!	Nesiya tova!	נְסִיעָה טוֹבָה !
Regards to the family!	Dash lamishpacha!	ד"ש לַמִּשְׁפָּחָה !
Hello! (only used when answering phone)	Allo!	הָלוֹ !
Bye!	Bai!	בַּיי !

Useful Words
Milim Shimushi'yot
מִלִים שִׁמוּשִׁיוֹת

🎧 MP3**4**

a little	ketzat	קְצָת
a lot	harbeh	הַרְבֵּה
again	od hapa'am	עוֹד הַפַּעַם
all	hakol	הַכֹּל
and	ve...	וְ...
in	be...	בְּ...
certainly	bevadai	בְּוַדַאי
correct	nachon	נָכוֹן
good	tov	טוֹב
here	po/kan	פֹּה/כָּאן
there	sham	שָׁם
Indeed?(!)	Be'emet?(!)	בֶּאֱמֶת? (!)
What?	Ma?	מַה?
maybe	ulai	אוּלַי
nothin' at all	klum	כְּלוּם

now	achshav	עַכְשָׁו
same thing	oto davar	אוֹתוֹ דָּבָר
this	zeh	זֶה
enough	maspik	מַסְפִּיק
also	gam	גַם
not yet	adayin lo	עֲדַיִן לֹא
only	rak	רַק
very nice	yafeh me'od	יָפֶה מְאֹד

🎧MP35

My First Conversation
Hasicha Harishona Sheli
הַשִׂיחָה הָרִאשׁוֹנָה שֶׁלִּי

What's new, Roni?	Ma chadash, Roni?	מַה חָדָשׁ רוֹנִי?
I'm learning Hebrew.	Ani lomed (lomedet) Ivrit.	אֲנִי לוֹמֵד (לוֹמֶדֶת) עִבְרִית.
Very nice, where?	Yafeh me'od, eifo?	יָפֶה מְאֹד, אֵיפֹה?

From the Easy Shmeezy Guide to Hebrew.	MehaEasy-Shmeezy Guide to Hebrew.	מֵהַאִיזִי שְׁמִיזִי גַּיְיד טוּ הִיבְּרוּ.
Is it actually easy?	Zeh be'emet kal?	זֶה בֶּאֱמֶת קַל?
Very easy.	Kal me'od.	קַל מְאֹד.
Good luck!	Behatzlacha!	בְּהַצְלָחָה!
We'll be in touch!	Nihyeh bekesher!	נִהְיֶה בְּקֶשֶׁר!

🎧 MP36

Everyday Expressions
Bituyim Yomyomiyim
בִּטּוּיִים יוֹמְיוֹמִיִּים

I know.	Ani yode'a (yoda'at).	אֲנִי יוֹדֵעַ (יוֹדַעַת).
I know already.	Ani kvar yode'a (yoda'at).	אֲנִי כְּבָר יוֹדֵעַ (יוֹדַעַת).

I don't know.	Ani lo yode'a (yoda'at).	אֲנִי לֹא יוֹדֵעַ (יוֹדַעַת).
I forgot.	Shachachti.	שָׁכַחְתִּי.
I don't remember.	Ani lo zocher (zocheret).	אֲנִי לֹא זוֹכֵר (זוֹכֶרֶת).
I want to buy.	Ani rotzeh (rotza) liknot.	אֲנִי רוֹצֶה (רוֹצָה) לִקְנוֹת.
I have.	Yesh li.	יֵשׁ לִי.
I don't have.	Ein li.	אֵין לִי.
Do you speak Hebrew?	Ata medaber (At medaberet) Ivrit?	אַתָּה מְדַבֵּר (אַתְּ מְדַבֶּרֶת) עִבְרִית?
I want to speak Hebrew.	Ani rotzeh (rotza) ledaber Ivrit.	אֲנִי רוֹצֶה (רוֹצָה) לְדַבֵּר עִבְרִית.
I'm now learning to speak.	Achshav ani lomed (lomedet) ledaber.	עַכְשָׁו אֲנִי לוֹמֵד (לוֹמֶדֶת) לְדַבֵּר.

Speak a little slower.	Tedaber (Tedabri) ketzat yoter le'at.	תְּדַבֵּר (תְּדַבְּרִי) קְצָת יוֹתֵר לְאַט.
It doesn't make a difference/ Never mind.	Lo meshaneh.	לֹא מְשַׁנֶּה.
Thank you very much.	Toda raba.	תּוֹדָה רַבָּה.
I think so.	Ani choshev (choshevet) sheken.	אֲנִי חוֹשֵׁב (חוֹשֶׁבֶת) שֶׁכֵּן.
I don't think so.	Ani choshev (choshevet) shelo.	אֲנִי חוֹשֵׁב (חוֹשֶׁבֶת) שֶׁלֹּא.
It seems so.	Nireh li sheken.	נִרְאֶה לִי שֶׁכֵּן.
Good luck!	Behatzlacha!	בְּהַצְלָחָה !
No difference.	Ein hevdel.	אֵין הֶבְדֵּל.
No doubt.	Ein safek.	אֵין סָפֵק
I understand.	Ani mevin (mevina).	אֲנִי מֵבִין (מְבִינָה).

I don't understand.	Ani lo mevin (mevina).	אֲנִי לֹא מֵבִין (מְבִינָה).
Say it again.	Tagid Shuv.	תַּגִּיד שׁוּב.
You're welcome.	Bivakasha.	בְּבַקָּשָׁה.
Go away.	Lech mikan.	לֵךְ מִכָּאן.
Leave me alone.	Ta'azov oti.	תַּעֲזֹב אוֹתִי.
Exactly!	Bediyuk!	בְּדִיּוּק !
Not like that.	Lo kacha.	לֹא כָּכָה.
What happened?	Ma kara?	מַה קָרָה ?
Make yourself at home.	Targish (Targishi) babayit.	תַּרְגִּישׁ (תַּרְגִּישִׁי) בַּבַּיִת.
Have a seat.	Shev (Sh'vi).	שֵׁב (שְׁבִי).
What in the world?! (lit. what suddenly)	Ma pitom?!	מַה פִּתְאוֹם ? ? !

What are you talkin' about?! (this expression means: Really?!)	Mah ata omer (at omeret)?!	מָה אַתָּה אוֹמֵר (אַתְּ אוֹמֶרֶת) ? !
The best!	Hachi tov!	הֲכִי טוֹב !

Question Words
Milot She'ela
מִלוֹת שְׁאֵלָה

🎧 MP3**7**

What?	Ma?	מַה ?
Where?	Eifo?	אֵיפֹה ?
Why?	Lama?	לָמָּה ?
When?	Matai?	מָתַי ?
How much?	Kama?	כַּמָּה ?
Who?	Mi?	מִי ?
Which?	Eizeh?	אֵיזֶה ?
How?	Eich?	אֵיךְ ?

28 ■ THE *EASY–SHMEEZY* GUIDE TO HEBREW

Common Questions
She'elot Metzuyot
שְׁאֵלוֹת מְצוּיוֹת

What is this?	Ma zeh?	? מַה זֶה
What happened?	Ma kara?	? מַה קָרָה
What are you doing?	Ma ata oseh (at osa)?	מָה אַתָּה עוֹשֶׂה (אַתְּ עוֹשָׂה) ?
What do you want?	Ma ata rotzeh (at rotza)?	מָה אַתָּה רוֹצֶה (אַתְּ רוֹצָה) ?
Where are ya' goin'?	Le'an ata holech (at holechet)?	לְאָן אַתָּה הוֹלֵךְ (אַתְּ הוֹלֶכֶת) ?
Where is there a Shul?	Eifo yesh beit keneset?	אֵיפֹה יֵשׁ בֵּית כְּנֶסֶת ?
Where is Mea Shearim?	Eifo zeh Me'a She'arim?	אֵיפֹה זֶה מֵאָה שְׁעָרִים ?
Where is Ben-Yehuda Street?	Eifo zeh Rechov Ben-Yehuda?	אֵיפֹה זֶה רְחוֹב בֶּן-יְהוּדָה ?

When does the tour start?	Matai matchil hatiyul?	מָתַי מַתְחִיל הַטִּיוּל?
When does the bus arrive?	Matai yagi'a ha'otobus?	מָתַי יַגִּיעַ הָאוֹטוֹבּוּס?
How much does this cost?	Kama zeh oleh?	כַּמָּה זֶה עוֹלֶה?
With whom are you going?	Im mi ata holech (at holechet)?	עִם מִי אַתָּה הוֹלֵךְ (אַתְּ הוֹלֶכֶת)?
Who is that?	Mi zeh (zot)?	מִי זֶה (זֹאת)?
How's the weather in America?	Eich mezeg ha'avir beAmerica?	אֵיךְ מֶזֶג הָאֲוִיר בְּאָמֶרִיקָה?
What's your name?	Ma hashem shelcha (shelach)?	מָה הַשֵּׁם שֶׁלְּךָ (שֶׁלָּךְ)?
How are you called?	Eich korim lecha (lach)?	אֵיךְ קוֹרְאִים לְךָ (לָךְ)?
Is there a...?	Yesh...?	יֵשׁ...?
Do you have a...?	Yesh licha (lach)...?	יֵשׁ לְךָ (לָךְ)...?

Why are you bothering me?	Lama ata (at) mafri'a li?	לָמָּה אַתָּה (אַתְּ) מַפְרִיעַ לִי?
How do you say internet in Hebrew?	Eich omrim internet be'Ivrit?	אֵיךְ אוֹמְרִים אִינְטֶרְנֶט בְּעִבְרִית?
How do you feel?	Eich ata margish (at margisha)?	אֵיךְ אַתָּה מַרְגִּישׁ (אַתְּ מַרְגִּישָׁה)?
Did you hear?	Shamata (Shamat)?	שָׁמַעְתָּ (שָׁמַעְתְּ)?

🎧 MP3 **9**

Questions for Conversation
She'elot Lesichot
שְׁאֵלוֹת לְשִׂיחָה

| What's your name? (lit. how are you called) | Eich korim licha (lach)? | אֵיךְ קוֹרְאִים לְךָ (לָךְ)? |
| Where are you studying? | Eifo ata lomed (at lomedet)? | אֵיפֹה אַתָּה לוֹמֵד (אַתְּ לוֹמֶדֶת)? |

Where do you live?	Eifo ata gar (at gara)?	אֵיפֹה אַתָּה גָּר (אַתְּ גָּרָה) ?
How old are you?	Ben kama ata (Bat kama at)?	בֶּן כַּמָּה אַתָּה (בַּת כַּמָּה אַתְּ) ?
Where were you born?	Eifo nolad'ta (noladet)?	אֵיפֹה נוֹלַדְתָּ (נוֹלַדְתְּ) ?
How many siblings do you have?	Kama achim yesh lecha (lach)?	כַּמָּה אַחִים יֵשׁ לְךָ (לָךְ) ?
Are you married?	Ata nasui (At nesu'a)?	אַתָּה נָשׂוּי (אַתְּ נְשׂוּאָה) ?
Do you have kids?	Yesh lecha (lach) yeladim?	יֵשׁ לְךָ (לָךְ) יְלָדִים ?
What do you do?	Bema ata osek (at oseket)?	בְּמָה אַתָּה עוֹסֵק (אַתְּ עוֹסֶקֶת) ?
How's it going at work?	Eich holech ba'avoda?	אֵיךְ הוֹלֵךְ בָּעֲבוֹדָה ?
How's the family?	Ma shlom hamishpacha?	מַה שְׁלוֹם הַמִּשְׁפָּחָה ?

Pronouns
Kinuyey Guf
כִּנּוּיֵי גּוּף

🎧 MP3 **10**

I	Ani	אֲנִי
you (m)	ata	אַתָּה
you (f)	at	אַתְּ
he	hu	הוּא
she	hi	הִיא
you (m,pl)	atem	אַתֶּם
you (f,pl)	aten	אַתֶּן
we	anachnu	אֲנַחְנוּ
they	hem	הֵם
they (f)	hen	הֵן

Possesive Pronouns
Kinuyei kinyan
כִּנּוּיֵי קִנְיָן

🎧 MP3 **11**

mine	sheli	שֶׁלִּי

your (m)	shelcha	שֶׁלְךָ
your (f)	shelach	שֶׁלָךְ
his	shelo	שֶׁלוֹ
her	shela	שֶׁלָה
your (m,pl)	shelchem	שֶׁלָכֶם
your (f,pl)	shelchen	שֶׁלָכֶן
our	shelanu	שֶׁלָנוּ
their (m)	shelhem	שֶׁלָהֶם
their (f)	shelhen	שֶׁלָהֶן

Nice to Meet You
Na'im Lehakir
נָעִים לְהַכִּיר

🎧 MP3 12

My name is Moshe Sherizen.	Sh'mi Moshe Sherizen.	שְׁמִי מֹשֶׁה שֶׁרִיזֶן.
I live in Jerusalem.	Ani gar BeYerushalayim.	אֲנִי גָּר בִּירוּשָׁלַיִם.

I've been living here for ten years.	Ani gar po kvar eser shanim.	אֲנִי גָּר פֹּה כְּבָר עֶשֶׂר שָׁנִים.
I was born in America.	Nolad'ti beAmerica.	נוֹלַדְתִּי בְּאַמֶרִיקָה.
My parents live in Detroit Michigan.	Hahorim sheli garim beDetroit Michigan.	הַהוֹרִים שֶׁלִּי גָּרִים בְּדֶטְרוֹיְט מִישִׁיגֶן.
I am 30 years old.	Ani ben shloshim.	אֲנִי בֶּן שְׁלוֹשִׁים.
I have three brothers and two sisters.	Yesh li shlosha achim ushtei achayot.	יֵשׁ לִי שְׁלוֹשָׁה אַחִים וּשְׁתֵּי אֲחָיוֹת.
I'm married.	Ani nasui.	אֲנִי נָשׂוּי.
I have four children.	Yesh li arba'a yeladim.	יֵשׁ לִי אַרְבָּעָה יְלָדִים.
I speak Hebrew.	Ani medaber Ivrit.	אֲנִי מְדַבֵּר עִבְרִית.
I like the language very much.	Ani me'od ohev et hasafa.	אֲנִי מְאֹד אוֹהֵב אֶת הַשָּׂפָה.

I teach Hebrew.	Ani melamed Ivrit.	אֲנִי מְלַמֵּד עִבְרִית.
If you'd like to learn together, send me an email.	Im ata rotzeh lilmod biyachad, shlach li meil.	אִם אַתָּה רוֹצֶה לִלְמֹד בְּיַחַד, שְׁלַח לִי מֵיְיל.
My email is: msherizen@gmail.com	Hameil sheli hu: msherizen@gmail.com	הַמֵּיְיל שֶׁלִּי הוּא: msherizen@gmail.com
It was nice to meet you!	Na'im lehakir!	נָעִים לְהַכִּיר!

I SCREAM. YOU SCREAM. WE ALL SCREAM FOR ICE CREAM! CHECK-OUT THIS COOL EXPRESSION. IN ISRAEL IF YOU SEE SOMEONE THREE TIMES IN A SHORT PERIOD OF TIME FOR EXAMPLE. IF YOU SEE YOUR BUDDY YONI IN THE MORNING AT THE KOTEL. THEN AT NOON IN MEA-SHEARIM AND THEN A THIRD TIME AT ANGEL'S BAKERY. UPON THE THIRD TIME YOU MIGHT HEAR HIM SAY "PA'AM SHLISHIT GLIDA" MEANING— THE THIRD TIME LET'S GO FOR ICE CREAM. NOW. HE DOESN'T REALLY WANT TO EAT ICE CREAM WITH YOU. IT'S MORE OF JUST A COOL WAY TO SAY "WHOA. I SAW YOU THREE TIMES TODAY...DUDE!"

SECTION TWO:
EXPAND

Now that you've begun speaking Hebrew with confidence and joy, let's expand your vocabulary to make you a more "sophistamicated" speaker. You'll learn words that'll help you at family get-togethers, while strolling around town, and even while taking the bus.

TIME DATE AND NUMBERS

🎧 MP3 13

The Days of the Week
Yemei Hashvu'a
יְמֵי הַשָּׁבוּעַ

Sunday	Yom Rishon	יוֹם רִאשׁוֹן
Monday	Yom Sheni	יוֹם שֵׁנִי
Tuesday	Yom Shlishi	יוֹם שְׁלִישִׁי
Wednesday	Yom Revi'i	יוֹם רְבִיעִי
Thursday	Yom Chamishi	יוֹם חֲמִישִׁי
Friday	Yom Shishi	יוֹם שִׁשִּׁי
Saturday	Shabbat	שַׁבָּת

🎧 MP3 14

Cardinal Numbers
Misparim Yisodiyim
מִסְפָּרִים יְסוֹדִיִּים

| 0 | efes | אֶפֶס |

1	achat	אַחַת
2	shtayim	שְׁתַּיִם
3	shalosh	שָׁלוֹשׁ
4	arba	אַרְבַּע
5	chamesh	חָמֵשׁ
6	shesh	שֵׁשׁ
7	sheva	שֶׁבַע
8	shmoneh	שְׁמוֹנֶה
9	tesha	תֵּשַׁע
10	eser	עֶשֶׂר
11	achad esreh	אַחַת עֶשְׂרֵה
12	shteim esreh	שְׁתֵּים עֶשְׂרֵה
13	shlosh esreh	שְׁלוֹשׁ עֶשְׂרֵה
14	arba esreh	אַרְבַּע עֶשְׂרֵה
15	chamesh esreh	חֲמֵשׁ עֶשְׂרֵה
16	shesh esreh	שֵׁשׁ עֶשְׂרֵה
17	shva esreh	שְׁבַע עֶשְׂרֵה
18	shmoneh esreh	שְׁמוֹנֶה עֶשְׂרֵה

19	tsha esreh	תְּשַׁע עֶשְׂרֵה
20	esrim	עֶשְׂרִים
21	esrim ve'achat	עֶשְׂרִים וְאַחַת
22	esrim veshtayim	עֶשְׂרִים וּשְׁתַּיִם
23	esrim veshalosh	עֶשְׂרִים וְשָׁלוֹשׁ
24	esrim ve'arba	עֶשְׂרִים וְאַרְבַּע
25	esrim vechamesh	עֶשְׂרִים וְחָמֵשׁ
30	shloshim	שְׁלוֹשִׁים
40	arba'im	אַרְבָּעִים
50	chamishim	חֲמִשִּׁים
60	shishim	שִׁשִּׁים
70	shivim	שִׁבְעִים
80	shmonim	שְׁמוֹנִים
90	tishim	תִּשְׁעִים
100	me'a	מֵאָה
200	matayim	מָאתַיִם
300	shlosh me'ot	שְׁלוֹשׁ מֵאוֹת

400	arba me'ot	אַרְבַּע מֵאוֹת
1,000	elef	אֶלֶף
2000	alpayim	אַלְפַּיִם
3000	shloshet alafim	שְׁלוֹשֶׁת אֲלָפִים
10,000	aseret alafim	עֲשֶׂרֶת אֲלָפִים
1,000,000	milyon	מִלְיוֹן

Ordinal Numbers
Misparim Siduri'im
מִסְפָּרִים סְדוּרִיִּים

🎧MP3**15**

first	rishon	רִאשׁוֹן
second	sheni	שֵׁנִי
third	shlishi	שְׁלִישִׁי
fourth	revi'i	רְבִיעִי
fifth	chamishi	חֲמִישִׁי
sixth	shishi	שִׁשִּׁי
seventh	shvi'i	שְׁבִיעִי
eighth	shmini	שְׁמִינִי

ninth	tish'i	תְּשִׁיעִי
tenth	asiri	עֲשִׂירִי

Time
Zman
זְמָן

early	mukdam	מֻקְדָּם
late	me'uchar	מְאֻחָר
time	zman	זְמָן
a long time	harbeh zman	הַרְבֵּה זְמָן
a little time	ketzat zman	קְצָת זְמָן
today	hayom	הַיּוֹם
in the morning	baboker	בַּבֹּקֶר
before noon	lifnei hatzaharayim	לִפְנֵי הַצָּהֳרַיִם
noon	tzaharayim	צָהֳרַיִם
afternoon	achrei hatzaharayim	אַחֲרֵי הַצָּהֳרַיִם

In the evening	ba'erev	בָּעֶרֶב
at night	balaila	בַּלַּיְלָה
tomorrow	machar	מָחָר
the day after tomorrow	machratayim	מָחֳרָתַיִם
yesterday	etmol	אֶתְמוֹל
two days ago	lifnei yomayim	שִׁלְשׁוֹם
day	yom	יוֹם
everyday	kol yom	כָּל־יוֹם
week	shavu'a	שָׁבוּעַ
weekend	sof shavu'a	סוֹף שָׁבוּעַ
month	chodesh	חֹדֶשׁ
year	shana	שָׁנָה
a couple of years	kama shanim	כַּמָּה שָׁנִים
this year	hashana hazot	הַשָּׁנָה הַזֹּאת
many years	harbeh shanim	הַרְבֵּה שָׁנִים
last year	hashana she'avra	הַשָּׁנָה שֶׁעָבְרָה

| next year | hashana haba'a | הַשָּׁנָה הַבָּאָה |
| two weeks ago | lifnei shvu'ayim | לִפְנֵי שְׁבוּעַיִם |

What Time is it?
Ma Hasha'a?
מָה הַשָּׁעָה?

moment	rega	רֶגַע
second	shniya	שְׁנִיָּה
minute	daka	דַּקָּה
What time is it?	Ma hasha'a?	מָה הַשָּׁעָה ?
It's 7:00.	Sha'a sheva.	שָׁעָה שֶׁבַע.
7:15	sheva vareva	שֶׁבַע וָרֶבַע
7:25	sheva esrim vechamesh	שֶׁבַע עֶשְׂרִים וְחָמֵשׁ
7:30	sheva vachetzi	שֶׁבַע וָחֵצִי
7:40	sheva ve'arba'im	שֶׁבַע וְאַרְבָּעִים

7:45	reva leshmoneh	רֶבַע לִשְׁמוֹנָה
It's 2 a.m.	hasha'a hi shtayim baboker.	הַשָּׁעָה הִיא שְׁתַּיִם בַּבֹּקֶר.
midnight	chatzot halaila	חֲצוֹת הַלַּיְלָה
He'll be coming in the afternoon.	Hu yavo batzaharayim.	הוּא יָבוֹא בַּצָּהֳרַיִם.
in two hours from now	be'od sha'atayim	בְּעוֹד שָׁעָתַיִם
two hours ago	lifnei sha'atayim	לִפְנֵי שָׁעָתַיִם
on time	bazman	בַּזְּמָן

DID YOU KNOW THAT THE UZI GUN WAS DEVELOPED BY ISRAELI MAJOR UZI GAL IN 1948? SINCE THEN MORE THAN 10 MILLION UZI MACHINE GUNS HAVE BEEN BUILT. MAJOR GAL PASSED AWAY IN 2002. HE DEFINITELY MADE A BIG IMPACT IN HIS LIFETIME.

PEOPLE ETC.

Family
Mishpacha
מִשְׁפָּחָה

🎧 MP3**18**

This is my_____.	Zeh (Zo) ha_____ sheli.	זֶה (זוֹ) הָ _____ שֶׁלִּי.
father	aba	אַבָּא
mother	ima	אִמָּא
parents	horim	הוֹרִים
brother	ach	אָח
sister	achot	אָחוֹת
daughter	bat	בַּת
son	ben	בֵּן
boy	yeled	יֶלֶד
girl	yalda	יַלְדָּה
children	yeladim	יְלָדִים
mother-in-law	chamot	חָמוֹת

father-in-law	choten/shver	חוֹתֵן/ שָׁוֶר
brother-in-law	gis	גִּיס
sister-in-law	gisa	גִּיסָה
daughter-in-law	kala	כַּלָּה
son-in-law	chatan	חָתָן
in-laws	mechutanim	מְחֻתָּנִים
husband	baal	בַּעַל
man	gever	גֶּבֶר
wife/woman	isha	אִשָּׁה
grandmother	savta	סַבְתָּא
grandfather	saba	סַבָּא
great grandfather	saba raba	סַבָּא רַבָּה
great grandmother	savta raba	סַבְתָּא רַבָּה
grandchild	neched	נֶכֶד
great-grandchild	nin	נִין
aunt	doda	דּוֹדָה

uncle	dod	דּוֹד
cousin	ben dod	בֶּן דּוֹד
nephew	achyan	אַחְיָן
niece	achyanit	אַחְיָנִית
My brother lives in the old city.	Ach sheli gar ba'Ir Ha'atika.	אָח שֶׁלִּי גָּר בָּעִיר הָעַתִּיקָה.
My grandpa is no longer young.	Saba sheli kvar lo tza'ir.	סַבָּא שֶׁלִּי כְּבָר לֹא צָעִיר.
The family is coming for Shabbos.	Hamishpacha magi'a leShabat.	הַמִּשְׁפָּחָה מַגִּיעָה לְשַׁבָּת.
He's the son-in-law of the prime minister.	Hu hechatan shel rosh hamemshala.	הוּא הֶחָתָן שֶׁל רֹאשׁ הַמֶּמְשָׁלָה.
Ooh-aah, such an illustrious father-in-law!	Ooh-ahh, choten kazeh chashuv.	אוּ-אַ, חוֹתֵן כָּזֶה חָשׁוּב.
My Uncle Dov is a dentist.	Dod sheli Dov, rofeh shinayim.	דּוֹד שֶׁלִּי דּוֹב, רוֹפֵא שִׁנַּיִם.

What's Your Profession?
Bema Ata Oved?
בְּמָה אַתָּה עוֹבֵד?

MP3 19

What do you do for a living?	Ma ata oseh (at osa) bachayim?	מָה אַתָּה עוֹשֶׂה (אַתְּ עוֹשָׂה) בַּחַיִּים?
What kinda work do you do?	Bema ata oved (at ovedet)?	בְּמָה אַתָּה עוֹבֵד (אַתְּ עוֹבֶדֶת)?
I am a...	Ani ...	...אֲנִי
student	student (studentit)	סְטוּדֶנְט (סְטוּדֶנְטִית)
teacher	moreh (mora)	מוֹרֶה (מוֹרָה)
doctor	rofeh (rof'a)	רוֹפֵא (רוֹפְאָה)
dentist	rofeh (rof'at) shinayim	רוֹפֵא (רוֹפְאַת) שְׁנַיִם
CEO	menahel (minahelet)	מְנַהֵל (מְנַהֶלֶת)
engineer	mehandes (mehandeset)	מְהַנְדֵּס (מְהַנְדֶּסֶת)

secretary (executive assistant)	mazkir (mazkira)	מַזְכִּיר (מַזְכִּירָה)
scientist	mad'an (ma'adanit)	מַדְעָן (מַדְעָנִית)
journalist	itonai (itona'it)	עִיתוֹנַאי (עִיתוֹנָאִית)
lawyer	orech (orechet) din	עוֹרֵךְ (עוֹרֶכֶת) דִּין
rabbi	rav	רַב
kollel scholar	avrech	אַבְרֵךְ
to profit	leharvi'ach	לְהַרְוִיחַ
money	kesef	כֶּסֶף
salary	maskoret	מַשְׂכֹּרֶת
I make a lot of money.	Ani marvi'ach (marvicha) harbeh kesef.	אֲנִי מַרְוִיחַ (מַרְוִיחָה) הַרְבֵּה כֶּסֶף.
I work at Uri's Pizza.	Ani oved (ovedet) bePizza Uri.	אֲנִי עוֹבֵד (עוֹבֶדֶת) בְּפִיצָה אוּרִי.

I work in a big office.	Ani oved (ovedet) bemisrad gadol.	אֲנִי עוֹבֵד (עוֹבֶדֶת) בְּמִשְׂרָד גָּדוֹל.
He wants to be a fireman.	Hu rotzeh lihyot kabai.	הוּא רוֹצֶה לִהְיוֹת כַּבַּאי.

	Feelings/Emotions *Regashot* רְגָשׁוֹת	🎧MP3**20**
How are you feeling?	Eich ata margish (at margisha)?	אֵיךְ אַתָּה מַרְגִּישׁ (אַתְּ מַרְגִּישָׁה)?
I'm...	Ani...	אֲנִי...
I am happy.	Ani same'ach (smecha).	אֲנִי שָׂמֵחַ (שְׂמֵחָה).
I'm fine.	Ani beseder.	אֲנִי בְּסֵדֶר.
I am sad.	Ani atzuv (atzuva).	אֲנִי עָצוּב (עֲצוּבָה).

I am pleased.	Ani merutzeh (merutza).	אֲנִי מְרֻצֶּה (מְרֻצָּה).
I am not pleased.	Ani lo merutzeh (merutza).	אֲנִי לֹא מְרֻצֶּה (מְרֻצָּה).
I am excited.	Ani metragesh (mitrageshet).	אֲנִי מִתְרַגֵּשׁ (מִתְרַגֶּשֶׁת).
I am worried.	Ani mud'ag (mud'eget).	אֲנִי מֻדְאָג (מֻדְאֶגֶת).
I am confused.	Ani mivulbal (mivulbelet).	אֲנִי מְבֻלְבָּל (מְבֻלְבֶּלֶת).
I am angry.	Ani ko'es (ko'eset).	אֲנִי כּוֹעֵס (כּוֹעֶסֶת).
I am scared.	Ani mefached (mefachedet).	אֲנִי מְפַחֵד (מְפַחֶדֶת).
I like...	Ani ohev (ohevet)...	אֲנִי אוֹהֵב (אוֹהֶבֶת)...
I don't like...	Ani lo ohev (ohevet)...	אֲנִי לֹא אוֹהֵב (אוֹהֶבֶת)...
I hate...	Ani soneh (sona'at)...	אֲנִי שׂוֹנֵא (שׂוֹנֵאת)...

I have energy.	Yesh li ko'ach.	יֵשׁ לִי כֹּחַ.
I don't have any energy.	Ein li ko'ach.	אֵין לִי כֹּחַ.
I am tired.	Ani ayeif (ayeifa).	אֲנִי עָיֵף (עֲיֵפָה).
I have regret.	Ani mitcharet (mitcharetet).	אֲנִי מִתְחָרֵט (מִתְחָרֶטֶת).
I am embarrassed.	Ani mitbayesh (mitbayeshet).	אֲנִי מִתְבַּיֵּשׁ (מִתְבַּיֶּשֶׁת).
I am insulted.	Ne'elavti.	נֶעֱלַבְתִּי.

DID YOU KNOW THAT... HEBREW IS THE LINGUA FRANCA OF JEWS ALL OVER THE WORLD? A LINGUA FRANCA IS A LANGUAGE SYSTEMATICALLY USED TO MAKE COMMUNICATION POSSIBLE BETWEEN PEOPLE WHO DON'T SHARE A MOTHER TONGUE. IN PARTICULAR WHEN IT IS A THIRD LANGUAGE. DISTINCT FROM BOTH MOTHER TONGUES.

GETTING AROUND

Finding Your Way
Eich Lehitmatzeh
אֵיךְ לְהִתְמַצֵּא

Where is...?	Eifo ha...?	אֵיפֹה הַ...?
Is it far from here?	Zeh rachok mikan?	זֶה רָחוֹק מִכָּאן?
Can I get there by foot?	Efshar lalechet lesham baregel?	אֶפְשָׁר לָלֶכֶת לְשָׁם בָּרֶגֶל?
How do I get to...?	Eich magi'im le...?	אֵיךְ מַגִּיעִים לְ...?
Straight ahead.	Yashar.	יָשָׁר.
Go all the way to the end.	Yashar yashar ad hasof.	יָשָׁר יָשָׁר עַד הַסּוֹף.
Take a right.	Yamina.	יָמִינָה.
Take a left.	Smola.	שְׂמֹאלָה.
At the traffic light.	Baramzor.	בָּרַמְזוֹר.
far	rachok	רָחוֹק

close	karov	קָרוֹב
north	tsafon	צָפוֹן
south	darom	דָּרוֹם
east	mizrach	מִזְרָח
west	ma'arav	מַעֲרָב

Transportation
Tachbura
תַּחְבּוּרָה

🎧MP3**22**

car	oto/rechev	אוֹטוֹ/ רֶכֶב
truck	masa'it	מַשָּׂאִית
motorcycle	ofano'a	אוֹפַנּוֹעַ
bicycle	ofanayim	אוֹפַנַּיִם
sidewalk	midracha	מִדְרָכָה
crosswalk	ma'avar chatzaya	מַעֲבַר חֲצָיָה
street	rechov	רְחוֹב
road	kvish	כְּבִישׁ

highway	kvish mahir	כְּבִישׁ מָהִיר
bridge	gesher	גֶּשֶׁר
tunnel	minhara	מִנְהָרָה
lane	netiv	נָתִיב
intersection	tzomet	צֹמֶת
stop light	ramzor	רַמְזוֹר
speed bump	pas he'ata	פַּס הָאֵטָה
new driver	nehag chadash	נֶהָג חָדָשׁ
driver's license	risheyon nehiga	רִשְׁיוֹן נְהִיגָה
He cut me off!	Hu akaf oti!	הוּא עָקַף אוֹתִי !
What a jerk!	Eizeh metoraf!	אֵיזֶה מְטוֹרָף !
Next time I'll take a cab	Pa'am habaa ani ekach monit.	פַּעַם הַבָּאָה אֲנִי אֶקַּח מוֹנִית.

On the Bus
Ba'otobus
בָּאוֹטוֹבּוּס

bus	otobus	אוֹטוֹבּוּס
bus stop	tachanat otobus	תַּחֲנַת אוֹטוֹבּוּס
central bus station	tachana merkazit	תַּחֲנָה מֶרְכָּזִית
bus pass	kartisiya	כַּרְטִיסִיָּה
bus card	rav kav	רַב קַו
youth pass	kartis no'ar	כַּרְטִיס נוֹעַר
adult pass	kartisiya regila	כַּרְטִיסִיָּה רְגִילָה
round trip	haloch vachazor	הָלוֹךְ וַחֲזוֹר
receipt	kabala	קַבָּלָה
front door	delet kidmit	דֶּלֶת קָדְמִית
back door	delet achorit	דֶּלֶת אֲחוֹרִית
Get on already, I wanna start driving.	Ta'aleh kvar, Ani rotzeh linso'a.	תַּעֲלֶה כְּבָר, אֲנִי רוֹצֶה לִנְסֹעַ.

Move, I'm closing the door.	Zuz, ani soger et hadelet.	זוז, אֲנִי סוֹגֵר אֶת הַדֶּלֶת.
Driver, wait a moment!	Nehag, rega!	נֶהָג, רֶגַע!
Driver, stop the bus!	Nehag ta'atzor!	נֶהָג תַּעֲצֹר!
Ask nicely.	Tevakesh yafeh.	תְּבַקֵשׁ יָפֶה.
Driver, please stop the bus!	Nehag, bevakasha la'atzor!	נֶהָג, בְּבַקָשָׁה לַעֲצֹר!
Please open the storage compartment!	Ta mit'an bevakasha!	תָּא מִטְעָן בְּבַקָשָׁה!
How much does a one-time ticket cost?	Kama oleh nesiya?	כַּמָה עוֹלָה נְסִיעָה?
Do you have change?	Yesh lecha odef?	יֵשׁ לְךָ עוֹדֶף?

Can you tell me where to get off for Har Hertzel?	Ata yachol lehagid li eifo laredet leHar Hertzel?	אַתָּה יָכוֹל לְהַגִּיד לִי אֵיפֹה לָרֶדֶת לְהַר הֶרְצֵל ?
Does this bus go to Tel Aviv?	Ha'otobus magi'a leTel Aviv?	הָאוֹטוֹבּוּס מַגִּיעַ לְתֵל אָבִיב ?
Where is the central bus station?	Eifo hatachana hamerkazit?	אֵיפֹה הַתַּחֲנָה הַמֶּרְכָּזִית ?
Driver, can you turn on the air conditioning.	Nahag, efshar lehaf'il mazgan?	נֶהַג, אֶפְשָׁר לְהַפְעִיל מַזְגָּן ?

DID YOU KNOW THAT IN ISRAEL IT IS VERY COMMON FOR A COMPLETE STRANGER TO INQUIRE ABOUT YOUR PERSONAL FINANCES? FOR EXAMPLE, THE GUY SITTING NEXT TO YOU ON A BUS MIGHT ASK YOU HOW MUCH MONEY YOU MAKE A MONTH OR HE MIGHT WANT TO KNOW IF YOU OWN/RENT YOUR APARTMENT. SOCIOLOGIST DR. E.Z. SHMEEZELEVSKY EXPLAINS THAT THIS BEHAVIOR IS DUE TO THE NATURAL SENSE OF BROTHERHOOD THAT IS FELT AMONGST ISRAELIS WHICH STEMS FROM THE PRINCIPLE OF "KOL YISRAEL AREIVIM ZEH LAZEH".

ME AND MY WORLD

	The Body *Haguf* הַגּוּף		🎧 MP3 24

body	guf	גּוּף
head	rosh	רֹאשׁ
face	panim	פָּנִים
forehead	metzach	מֵצַח
eye	ayin	עַיִן
eyebrows	gabot	גַּבּוֹת
ear	ozen	אֹזֶן
nose	af	אַף
mouth	pe	פֶּה
lips	sfatayim	שְׂפָתַיִם
cheek	lechi	לְחִי
teeth	shinayim	שִׁנַּיִם
tongue	lashon	לָשׁוֹן
hair	se'ar	שֵׂעָר

moustache	safam	שָׂפָם
beard	zakan	זָקָן
neck	tzavar	צַוָּאר
shoulder	katef	כָּתֵף
back	gav	גַּב
heart	lev	לֵב
belly	beten	בֶּטֶן
arm	zro'a	זְרוֹעַ
hand	yad	יָד
finger	etzba	אֶצְבַּע
thigh	yarech	יָרֵךְ
knee	berech	בֶּרֶךְ
foot	regel	רֶגֶל
nail	tziporen	צִפֹּרֶן
bone	etzem	עֶצֶם
blood	dam	דָּם
My hand hurts.	Ko'ev li hayad.	כּוֹאֵב לִי הַיָּד.
Call a doctor.	K'ra lerofeh.	קְרָא לְרוֹפֵא.

My Clothes
Hab'gadim Sheli
הַבְּגָדִים שֶׁלִּי

I wear my _____.	Ani lovesh (loveshet) et ha_____ sheli.	אֲנִי לוֹבֵשׁ (לוֹבֶשֶׁת) אֶת הַ_____ שֶׁלִּי.
underwear	tachtonim	תַּחְתּוֹנִים
hat	kova	כּוֹבַע
shirt	chultza	חֻלְצָה
tie	aniva	עֲנִיבָה
pants	michnasayim	מִכְנָסַיִם
pocket	kis	כִּיס
belt	chagora	חֲגוֹרָה
dress	simla	שִׂמְלָה
socks	garbayim	גַּרְבַּיִם
shoes	na'alayim	נַעֲלַיִם
suit	chalifa	חֲלִיפָה
coat	me'il	מְעִיל

scarf	tza'if	צָעִיף
gloves	k'fafot	כְּפָפוֹת
boots	magafayim	מַגָּפַיִם
skullcap	kipa	כִּפָּה
knit skullcap	kipa sruga	כִּפָּה סְרוּגָה
On Shabbos they wear their nicest clothes.	BeShabat hem lovshim et habegadim hachi yafim shelhem.	בְּשַׁבָּת הֵם לוֹבְשִׁים אֶת הַבְּגָדִים הֲכִי יָפִים שֶׁלָּהֶם.
I only want to buy clothes at Mamila.	Ani rotzeh (rotza) liknot begadim rak beMamila.	אֲנִי רוֹצֶה (רוֹצָה) לִקְנוֹת בְּגָדִים רַק בְּמַמִּילָא.

🎧 MP3 **26**

My Stuff
Hachafatzim Sheli
הַחֲפָצִים שֶׁלִּי

glasses	mishkafayim	מִשְׁקָפַיִם
keys	maftechot	מַפְתְּחוֹת

money	kesef	כֶּסֶף
wallet	arnak	אַרְנָק
purse	tik	תִּיק
pocket	kis	כִּיס
pen	et	עֵט
pencil	iparon	עִפָּרוֹן
notebook	machberet	מַחְבֶּרֶת
paper	niyar	נְיָר
books	sfarim	סְפָרִים
newspaper	iton	עִתּוֹן
watch	sha'on yad	שָׁעוֹן
toys	mischakim	מִשְׂחָקִים
car	rechev	רֶכֶב
tools	klei avoda	כְּלֵי עֲבוֹדָה
friends	chaverim	חֲבֵרִים
Yaffa has a lot of friends.	LeYaffa yesh harbeh chaverim.	לְיָפָה יֵשׁ הַרְבֵּה חֲבֵרִים.

I need money to buy a new car.	Ani tzarich kesef liknot rechev chadash.	אֲנִי צָרִיךְ כֶּסֶף לִקְנוֹת רֶכֶב חָדָשׁ.

	The House *Habayit* הַבַּיִת	🎧 MP3 **27**
house/home	bayit	בַּיִת
room	cheder	חֶדֶר
wall	kir	קִיר
door	delet	דֶּלֶת
floor	ritzpa	רִצְפָּה
ceiling	tikra	תִּקְרָה
window	chalon	חַלּוֹן
stairs	madregot	מַדְרֵגוֹת
attic	boydem	בּוֹיְדֶעם
roof	gag	גַּג
balcony	mirpeset	מִרְפֶּסֶת

basement	martef	מַרְתֵּף
yard	chatzer	חָצֵר
garden	gina	גִּנָּה
kitchen	mitbach	מִטְבָּח
living room	salon	סָלוֹן
bathroom	sherutim	שֵׁרוּתִים
bedroom	chadar sheina	חֲדַר שֵׁנָה
Yosef has a big house.	LeYosef yesh bayit gadol.	לְיוֹסֵף יֵשׁ בַּיִת גָּדוֹל.
Close the window.	S'gor et hachalon.	סְגוֹר אֶת הַחַלּוֹן

MP328

Furniture
Rihut
רִהוּט

closet	aron	אָרוֹן
drawer	megera	מְגֵרָה
bed	mita	מִטָּה

SECTION TWO: EXPAND ▪ 67

pillow	karit	כָּרִית
blanket	smicha	שְׂמִיכָה
table	shulchan	שֻׁלְחָן
chair	kiseh	כִּסֵּא
bench	safsal	סַפְסָל
couch	sapa	סַפָּה
book shelf	aron sfarim	אֲרוֹן סְפָרִים
lights	te'ura	תְּאוּרָה
electric outlet	sheka	שֶׁקַע
fan	me'avrer	מְאַוְרֵר
furniture	rihut	רִהוּט
I want to buy new furniture.	Ani rotzeh liknot rihut chadash.	אֲנִי רוֹצֶה לִקְנוֹת רִהוּט חָדָשׁ.

	In the Kitchen *Bamitbach* בַּמִּטְבָּח	🎧 MP3 29
pot	sir	סִיר

pan	machvat	מַחֲבַת
sink	kiyor	כִּיּוֹר
counter	shayesh	שַׁיִשׁ
faucet	berez	בֶּרֶז
oven	tanur	תַּנּוּר
stove	kirayim	כִּירַיִם
kettle	kumkum	קָמְקוּם
garbage can	pach	פַּח
table	shulchan	שֻׁלְחָן
chair	kiseh	כִּסֵּא
plate	tzalachat	צַלַּחַת
ladle	matzeket	מַצֶּקֶת
tray	magash	מַגָּשׁ
towel	magevet	מַגֶּבֶת
napkin	mapiyon	מַפִּיוֹן
fork	mazleg	מַזְלֵג
knife	sakin	סַכִּין
spoon	kaf	כַּף
sugar	sukar	סֻכָּר

salt	melach	מֶלַח
salt shaker	milchiya	מִלְחִיָּה

	Telephone *Telefon* טֶלֶפוֹן	🎧MP3**30**
cell phone	telefon nayad/ pelefon	טֶלֶפוֹן נַיָּד/ פֶּלֶאפוֹן
text message	sms	אֶס. אֶם. אֶס.
ring	tziltzul	צִלְצוּל
pound	sulamit	סוּלָמִית
star	kochavit	כּוֹכָבִית
voice mail	ta hakoli	תָּא הַקּוֹלִי
Who is this?	Mi zeh?	מִי זֶה ?
This is Moshe speaking	Medaber Moshe.	מְדַבֵּר מֹשֶׁה.
What's doing?	Ma ha'inyanim?	מָה הָעִנְיָנִים ?

Can I speak with Yossi?	Efshar ledaber im Yossi?	אֶפְשָׁר לְדַבֵּר עִם יוֹסִי ?
He can't speak now.	Hu lo yachol ledaber achshav.	הוּא לֹא יָכוֹל לְדַבֵּר עַכְשָׁו.
Is the matter urgent?	Zeh dachuf?	זֶה דָּחוּף ?
Try later.	Tenaseh me'uchar yoter.	תְּנַסֶּה מְאֻחָר יוֹתֵר.
Call me tomorrow.	Titkasher elai machar.	תִּתְקַשֵּׁר אֵלַי מָחָר.
You want to leave a message?	Rotzeh lehash'ir hoda'a?	רוֹצֶה לְהַשְׁאִיר הוֹדָעָה ?
No thanks.	Lo toda.	לֹא תּוֹדָה.
He won't call you back anyway.	Bechol ofen hu lo yachzor elecha.	בְּכָל-אוֹפֶן הוּא לֹא יַחֲזֹר אֵלֶיךָ.
We'll be in touch.	Nihyeh bekesher.	נִהְיֶה בְּקֶשֶׁר.

Hi, you've reached the voicemail of Rami Levi, please leave a message after the tone.	Shalom, higatem lata hakoli shel Rami Levi, na lehash'ir hoda'a acharei hatzlil.	שָׁלוֹם הִגַּעְתֶּם לַתָּא הַקּוֹלִי שֶׁל רָמִי לֵוִי, נָא לְהַשְׁאִיר הוֹדָעָה אַחֲרֵי הַצְּלִיל.
For hebrew press 1.	Le'Ivrit hakishu achat.	לְעִבְרִית הַקִּישׁוּ אַחַת.
For Arabic press 2.	Al Arabia wallaballa tnen.	אֶל עֲרַבְּיָא וַואלַאבַּאלַּא תְּנֵין.
For english press 3.	Forrr Inglish press sree.	פוֹר אִינְגְלִישׁ פְּרֶס סְרִי.
For Yiddish press 4.	Far Yidish drik fir.	פַאר יִידִישׁ דרוק פִיר.

WHAT DO ISRAELI COWS SAY? EMMMOOOOOOOOO! (SEE PAGE 149)

FOOD STUFF

	Food *Ochel* אוֹכֶל	🎧 MP3 31
breakfast	aruchat boker	אֲרוּחַת בֹּקֶר
lunch	aruchat tzaharayim	אֲרוּחַת צָהֳרַיִם
dinner	aruchat erev	אֲרוּחַת עֶרֶב
He eats a lot of…	Hu ochel harbeh…	הוּא אֹכֵל הַרְבֵּה...
She loves to eat…	Hi ohevet le'echol…	הִיא אוֹהֶבֶת לֶאֱכֹל...
bread	lechem	לֶחֶם
roll	lachmaniya	לַחְמָנִיָּה
sandwich	karich/ sendvitsh	כָּרִיךְ\סֶנְדְּוִויץ'
cookie	ugiya	עֻגִּיָּה
cake	uga	עֻגָה
eggs	beitzim	בֵּיצִים

butter	chema	חֶמְאָה
cheese	gvina	גְּבִינָה
noodles	itri'ot	אָטְרִיּוֹת
rice	orez	אוֹרֶז
salad	salat	סָלָט
soup	marak	מָרָק
meat	basar	בָּשָׂר
fish	dag	דָּג
chicken	ohf	עוֹף
turkey	hodu	הוֹדוּ
falafel	falafel	פָלָאפֶל
hummus	chumus	חוּמוּס
crackers	krekerim	קְרֶקֶרִים
pretzels	beigalach	בֵּייגְלַךְ
junk-food	chatifim	חֲטִיפִים
sunflower seeds	gar'inim	גַּרְעִינִים
What does he want to eat?	Ma hu rotzeh le'echol?	מָה הוּא רוֹצֶה לֶאֱכוֹל ?

I want to eat borekas.	Ani rotzeh (rotza) le'echol burekas.	אֲנִי רוֹצֶה (רוֹצָה) לֶאֱכוֹל בּוּרֶקַס.
I'm hungry.	Ani ra'ev (re'eva).	אֲנִי רָעֵב (רְעֵבָה).
She loves restaurants.	Hi ohevet mis'adot.	הִיא אוֹהֶבֶת מִסְעָדוֹת.

🎧MP3 **32**

Drinks
Shtiya
שְׁתִיָּה

Give me a glass of...	Ten li kos...	תֵּן לִי כּוֹס...
water	mayim	מַיִם
milk	chalav	חָלָב
juice	mitz	מִיץ
tea	tei	תֵּה
coffee	kafeh	קָפֶה
cola	kola	קוֹלָה

wine	yayin	יַיִן
beer	bira	בִּירָה
liquor	mashkeh charif	מַשְׁקֶה חָרִיף
cold drink	shtiya kara	שְׁתִיָּה קָרָה
hot drink	shtiya chama	שְׁתִיָּה חַמָּה
I'm thirsty.	Ani tzameh (tzme'a).	אֲנִי צָמֵא (צְמֵאָה).
He's a little drunk.	Hu ketzat shikur.	הוּא קְצָת שִׁכּוֹר.

MP3 33

Fruit
Peirot
פֵּרוֹת

I like to eat...	Ani ohev (ohevet) le'echol...	אֲנִי אוֹהֵב (אוֹהֶבֶת) לֶאֱכוֹל...
apple	tapu'ach	תַּפּוּחַ
apricot	mishmesh	מִשְׁמֵשׁ
banana	banana	בַּנָנָה

pear	agas	אַגָּס
orange	tapuz	תַּפּוּז
grapefruit	eshkolit	אֶשְׁכּוֹלִית
plum	shezif	שְׁזִיף
peach	afarsek	אֲפַרְסֵק
grapes	anavim	עֲנָבִים
lemon	limon	לִימוֹן
pomegranate	rimon	רִמּוֹן
fig	te'ena	תְּאֵנָה
date	tamar	תָּמָר
berry	tut	תּוּת
cherry	duvdevan	דּוּבְדְּבָן
olive	zayit	זַיִת
melon	melon	מֶלוֹן
almonds	shkedim	שְׁקֵדִים
nuts	egozim	אֱגוֹזִים
In the shuk there many kinds of fruits.	Bashuk yesh harbeh sugei peirot.	בַּשּׁוּק יֵשׁ הַרְבֵּה סוּגֵי פֵּרוֹת.

Vegetables
Yerakot
יְרָקוֹת

potato	tapu'ach adama	תַּפּוּחַ אֲדָמָה
cucumber	melafefon	מְלָפְפוֹן
tomato	agvaniya	עַגְבָנִיָּה
carrot	gezer	גֶּזֶר
onion	batzal	בָּצָל
garlic	shum	שׁוּם
beans	sha'u'it	שְׁעוּעִית
cabbage	kruv	כְּרוּב
radish	tznon	צְנוֹן
pepper	pilpel	פִּלְפֵּל
squash	dla'at	דְּלַעַת
celery	seleri	סֶלֶרִי
mushrooms	pitriyot	פִּטְרִיּוֹת
sprouts	nevatim	נְבָטִים

| It's healthy to eat vegetables. | Zeh bari le'echol yerakot. | זֶה בָּרִיא לֶאֱכוֹל יְרָקוֹת. |
| Mother cooks potatoes with onions. | Ima mevashelet tapu'ach im batzal. | אִמָּא מְבַשֶּׁלֶת תַּפּוּחַ אֲדָמָה עִם בָּצָל. |

THE WORLD

In the City
Ba'ir
בָּעִיר

🎧 MP3 35

house	bayit	בַּיִת
houses	batim	בָּתִּים
street	rachov	רְחוֹב
sidewalk	midracha	מִדְרָכָה
gate	gader	גָּדֵר
building	binyan	בִּנְיָן

school	beit sefer	בֵּית סֵפֶר
synagogue	beit keneset	בֵּית כְּנֶסֶת
garden	gina	גִּנָּה
bench	safsal	סַפְסָל
bicycle	ofanayim	אוֹפַנַּיִם
bus	otobus	אוֹטוֹבּוּס
airplane	matos	מָטוֹס
police	mishtara	מִשְׁטָרָה
stores	chanuyot	חֲנֻיּוֹת

The Weather
Mezeg Ha'avir
מֶזֶג הָאֲוִיר

🎧 MP3**36**

| How's the weather? | Eich mezeg ha'avir? | מַה מֶזֶג הָאֲוִיר? |
| What's the temperature in Eilat? | Ma hatemperatura be'Eilat? | מָה הַטֶּמְפֶּרָטוּרָה בְּאֵילַת? |

The weather is...	Mezeg ha'avir hu...	מֶזֶג הָאֲוִיר הוּא...
nice	yafe/na'im	יָפֶה/נָעִים
not good	lo tov	לֹא טוֹב
fine	beseder	בְּסֵדֶר
cold	kar	קַר
cool	karir	קָרִיר
hot	cham	חַם
humid	lach	לַח
cloudy	me'unan	מְעֻנָּן
foggy	arafel	מְעֻרְפָּל
sunny	bahir	בָּהִיר
forecast	tachazit	תַּחֲזִית
It's raining.	Yored geshem.	יוֹרֵד גֶּשֶׁם.
It's stormy outside.	So'er bachutz.	סוֹעֵר בַּחוּץ.
It's snowing. (this phrase is not commonly used)	Yored sheleg.	יוֹרֵד שֶׁלֶג.

There's a strong wind blowing.	Yesh ru'ach chazaka.	יֵשׁ רוּחַ חֲזָקָה.
Hi grandma, how's the weather in Miami?	Hi savta, eich mezeg ha'avir beMiami?	הַי סַבְתָּא, אֵיךְ מֶזֶג הָאֲוִיר בְּמַיַאמִי ?
In Israel it doesn't rain in the summer.	BeYisra'el lo yored geshem bakayitz.	בְּיִשְׂרָאֵל לֹא יוֹרֵד גֶּשֶׁם בַּקַּיִץ.
thunder	ra'am	רַעַם
lightning	barak	בָּרָק
rainbow	keshet	קֶשֶׁת
winter	choref	חֹרֶף
summer	kayitz	קַיִץ
spring	aviv	אָבִיב
fall	stav	סְתָיו

Nature
Teva
טֶבַע

What a ...	Eizeh ...	אֵיזֶה...
sky	shamayim	שָׁמַיִם
land	eretz	אֶרֶץ
grass	desheh	דֶּשֶׁא
field	sadeh	שָׂדֶה
tree	etz	עֵץ
roots	sharashim	שָׁרָשִׁים
tree trunk	geza	גֶּזַע
branches	anafim	עֲנָפִים
waterfall	mapal	מַפָּל
river	nahar	נָהָר
natural spring	ma'eyan	מַעְיָן
lake	agam	אֲגַם
sea	yam	יָם
mountain	har	הַר

beach	chof	חוֹף
sand	chol	חוֹל
sun	shemesh	שֶׁמֶשׁ
moon	yare'ach	יָרֵחַ
stars	kochavim	כּוֹכָבִים
clouds	ananim	עֲנָנִים
air	avir	אֲוִיר
wind	ru'ach	רוּחַ
storm	se'ara	סְעָרָה
flowers	prachim	פְּרָחִים
vegetation	tzmachim	צְמָחִים
stones	avanim	אֲבָנִים
mud	botz	בּוֹץ
flood	mabul	מַבּוּל
earthquake	re'idat adama	רְעִידַת אֲדָמָה

	Animals *Chayot* חַיּוֹת	MP3 38
lion	aryeh	אַרְיֵה
monkey	kof	קוֹף
bear	dov	דֹּב
elephant	pil	פִּיל
tiger	namer	נָמֵר
camel	gamal	גָּמָל
fox	shu'al	שׁוּעָל
snake	nachash	נָחָשׁ
cow	para	פָּרָה
horse	sus	סוּס
donkey	chamor	חֲמוֹר
sheep	keves	כֶּבֶשׂ
dog	kelev	כֶּלֶב
cat	chatula	חֲתוּלָה
duck	barvaz	בַּרְוָז
goose	avaz	אַוָּז

frog	tzfardei'a	צְפַרְדֵּעַ
bird	tzipor	צִפּוֹר
fish	dag	דָּג
deer	tzvi	צְבִי
My son loves the zoo.	Haben sheli ohev et gan hachayot.	הַבֵּן שֶׁלִּי אוֹהֵב אֶת גַּן הַחַיּוֹת.
I prefer the petting zoo.	Ani ma'adif et pinat hachai.	אֲנִי מַעֲדִיף אֶת פִּנַּת הַחַי.

🎧 MP3 39

Colors
Tzva'im
צְבָעִים

What color is this?	Eizeh tzeva zeh?	אֵיזֶה צֶבַע זֶה ?
This is blue.	Zeh kachol.	זֶה כָּחֹל.
white	lavan	לָבָן
black	shachor	שָׁחֹר
red	adom	אָדֹם

blue	kachol	כָּחֹל
yellow	tzahov	צָהֹב
green	yarok	יָרֹק
orange	katom	כָּתֹם
purple	segol	סָגוֹל
pink	varod	וָרֹד
brown	chum	חוּם
gold	zahav	זָהָב
silver	kesef	כֶּסֶף
gray	afor	אָפֹר
light	bahir	בָּהִיר
dark	keheh	כֵּהֶה
My favorite color is blue.	Hatzeva she'ani hachi ohev hu kachol.	הַצֶּבַע שֶׁאֲנִי הֲכִי אוֹהֵב הוּא כָּחֹל.
The grass is green.	Hadesheh yarok.	הַדֶּשֶׁא יָרֹק.
The flag is blue and white.	Hadegel kachol velavan.	הַדֶּגֶל כָּחֹל וְלָבָן.

Politics
Politika
פּוֹלִיטִיקָה

government	memshala	מֶמְשָׁלָה
parliament	knesset	כְּנֶסֶת
prime minister	rosh hamemshala	רֹאשׁ הַמֶּמְשָׁלָה
president	nasi	נָשִׂיא
minister	sar	שַׂר
member of parliament	chaver keneset	חָבֵר כְּנֶסֶת
mayor	rosh ha'ir	רֹאשׁ הָעִיר
propaganda	ta'amula	תַּעֲמוּלָה
coalition	ko'alitzi'a	קוֹאָלִיצְיָה
election	bechirot	בְּחִירוֹת
vote	lehatzbi'a	לְהַצְבִּיעַ
Who are you voting for?	Lemi ata matzbi'a?	לְמִי אַתָּה מַצְבִּיעַ?
Are you voting?	Ata matzbi'a?	אַתָּה מַצְבִּיעַ?

My vote doesn't make a difference.	Hakol sheli lo mashpi'a.	הַקוֹל שֶׁלִי לֹא מַשְׁפִּיעַ.
If everyone said that...	Im kol echad haya omer et zeh...	אִם כָּל-אֶחָד הָיָה אוֹמֵר אֶת זֶה...
Dude, I'm not an Israeli citizen, I can't vote.	Achi, ani lo Yisre'eli, ani lo yachol lehatzbi'a.	אָחִי, אֲנִי לֹא יִשְׂרָאֵלִי, אֲנִי לֹא יָכוֹל לְהַצְבִּיעַ.

MP3 41

High-Tech
Hai-Tek
הַיי–טֶק

technology	technologiya	טֶכְנוֹלוֹגְיָה
computer	machshev	מַחְשֵׁב
laptop	machshev nayad	מַחְשֵׁב נַיָד
mouse	achbar	עַכְבָּר
keyboard	mikledet	מִקְלֶדֶת

screen	masach	מָסָךְ
program	tochna	תּוֹכְנָה
email	meil	מֵייל
password	sisma	סִסְמָא
website	atar	אֲתָר
homepage	daf habayit	דַּף הַבַּיִת
link	kishur	קִשּׁוּר
search engine	mano'a chipus	מָנוֹעַ חִפּוּשׂ
to surf	liglosh	לִגְלשׁ
It's not worth surfing without a filter.	Lo kedai leglosh beli sinun.	לֹא כְּדַאי לִגְלשׁ בְּלִי סִנּוּן.

GOOD TO KNOW

Don't Forget These
Al Tishkach et Elu
אַל תִּשְׁכַּח אֶת אֵלוּ

Come here.	Bo lepo.	בּוֹא לְפֹה.
That's not cool./That's not okay.	Zeh lo beseder.	זֶה לֹא בְּסֵדֶר.
I don't have any time.	Ein li zman.	אֵין לִי זְמָן.
That's how it goes.	Kacha zeh holech.	כָּכָה זֶה הוֹלֵךְ.
truthfully	be'emet	בֶּאֱמֶת
Have a look.	Tistakel (Tistakli).	תִּסְתַּכֵּל (תִּסְתַּכְּלִי).
Listen in.	Takshiv (Takshivi).	תַּקְשִׁיב (תַּקְשִׁיבִי).
the way it should be	kimo shetzarich	כְּמוֹ שֶׁצָּרִיךְ

It's not your business.	Zeh lo ha'esek shelcha (shelach).	זֶה לֹא הָעֵסֶק שֶׁלְּךָ (שֶׁלָּךְ).
Where're you from?	Me'eifo ata (at)?	מֵאֵיפֹה אַתָּה (אַתְּ) ?
Do you know Marry Poppins?	Ata makir (At makira) et Marry Poppins?	אַתָּה מַכִּיר (אַתְּ מַכִּירָה) אֶת מֶרִי פּוֹפִּינְס ?
Yeah, sure I know her.	Ken, betach she'ani makir (makira).	כֵּן, בֶּטַח שֶׁאֲנִי מַכִּיר (מַכִּירָה).
We grew up together.	Gadalnu beyachad.	גָּדַלְנוּ בְּיַחַד.
Be quiet!	Sheket!	שֶׁקֶט !
Wait a second.	Chakeh rega.	חַכֵּה רֶגַע.
Don't bother me.	Al tafri'a li.	אַל תַּפְרִיעַ לִי.

Expressions and Slang
Bituyim U'sleng
בִּטּוּיִים וּסְלֶנְג

Don't exaggerate!	Lo lehagzim!	לֹא לְהַגְזִים !
It's very very good! (lit. somethin' somethin')	Masheu masheu!	מַשֶּׁהוּ מַשֶּׁהוּ !
In your dreams.	Bachalomot.	בַּחֲלוֹמוֹת.
No way Jose.	Ein matzav.	אֵין מַצָּב.
Unbelievable.	Lo ye'uman.	לֹא יֵאָמֵן.
Can't be.	Lo yitachen.	לֹא יִתָּכֵן.
It's only talk.	Zeh rak diburim.	זֶה רַק דִּבּוּרִים.
Awesome!	Madhim!	מַדְהִים !
Whoa!	Wai wai!	וַיי וַיי !
With pleasure!	Bekeif!	בְּכֵיף !
from A to Z	me'alef ad tav	מֵאָלֶף עַד תָּיו

last but not least	achron achron chaviv	אַחֲרוֹן אַחֲרוֹן חָבִיב
by the way	derech agav	דֶּרֶךְ אַגַּב
the straw that broke the camel's back	hakash sheshavar et gav hagamal	הַקַּשׁ שֶׁשָּׁבַר אֶת גַּב הַגָּמָל
That's it.	Zehu zeh.	זֶהוּ זֶה.
unusual	yotzeh dofen	יוֹצֵא דֹפֶן
time will tell	yamim yagidu	יָמִים יַגִּידוּ
cream of the crop	salta veshamna	סָלְתָּה וְשַׁמְנָה
the cherry on the cream	haduvdevan shebakatzefet	הַדּוּבְדְּבָן שֶׁבַּקַּצֶפֶת
I'll scratch your back you scratch mine.	Shmor li, eshmor licha.	שְׁמוֹר לִי, אֶשְׁמוֹר לָךְ.
I've had it.	Nishbar li.	נִשְׁבַּר לִי.
He's got a screw loose.	Nafal lo boreg.	נָפַל לוֹ בֹּרֶג.
What do I care?	Ma ichpat li?	מָה אִכְפַּת לִי?
horrible	al hapanim	עַל הַפָּנִים

nonsense	shtuyot	שְׁטֻיּוֹת
totally awesome (lit. a waste of time)	chaval al hazman	חֲבָל עַל הַזְּמַן
excellent	p'tzatza	פְּצָצָה
sweetheart	neshama	נְשָׁמָה
goodbye (the cool way of saying goodbye)	yala bai	יַאלְלָה בַּיי

Warning: The following expressions are not so polite...actually they're quite rude. I was contemplating whether or not to put them in the book because I'm a nice guy and this is a nice book and you are probably nice too. However, in the end I decided to put them so that way if you hear someone saying them you might want to think twice about becoming friends with them.

| Look for your friends. (meaning- Don't bother me!) | Chapes et hachaverim shelcha. | חַפֵּשׂ אֶת הַחֲבֵרִים שֶׁלְּךָ. |

If you don't have anything to do, don't do it here. (meaning- Get lost!)	Im ein lecha ma la'asot, al ta'ase et zeh po.	אִם אֵין לְךָ מַה לַעֲשׂוֹת, אַל תַּעֲשֶׂה אֶת זֶה פֹּה.
Stop making me crazy.	Tafsik (Tafsiki) leshage'a li et hasechel.	תַּפְסִיק (תפסיקי) לְשַׁגֵּעַ לִי אֶת הַשֵּׂכֶל.
What an idiot!	Eizeh Tipesh	אֵיזֶה טִפֵּשׁ !

Adjectives
Milot To'ar
מִלּוֹת תֹּאַר

It's...	Zeh...	זֶה...
bad	ra	רַע
big	gadol	גָּדוֹל
broken	shavur	שָׁבוּר
cheap	zol	זוֹל
clean	naki	נָקִי

closed	sagur	סָגוּר
cold	kar	קַר
complete	shalem	שָׁלֵם
difficult	kasheh	קָשֶׁה
dirty	meluchlach	מְלֻכְלָךְ
dry	yavesh	יָבֵשׁ
easy/easy-shmeezy	kal	קַל
empty	reik	רֵיק
expensive	yakar	יָקָר
fast	maher	מַהֵר
full	maleh	מָלֵא
good	tov	טוֹב
great	metzuyan	מְצֻיָּן
hard	kasheh	קָשֶׁה
horrible	al hapanim	עַל הַפָּנִים
hot	cham	חָם
important	chashuv	חָשׁוּב
interesting	me'anyen	מְעַנְיֵן

long	aroch	אָרוֹךְ
loose	rafui	רָפוּי
low	namuch	נָמוּךְ
new	chadash	חָדָשׁ
pleasent	na'im	נָעִים
normal	normali	נוֹרְמָלִי
old	yashan	יָשָׁן
open	patu'ach	פָּתוּחַ
poor	ani	עָנִי
rich	ashir	עָשִׁיר
short	katzar	קָצָר
slowly	le'at	לְאַט
small	katan	קָטָן
soft	rach	רַךְ
strange	muzar	מוּזָר
strong	chazak	חָזָק
tall	gavoha	גָּבוֹהַּ
tasty	ta'im	טָעִים
thick	aveh	עָבֶה

thin	dak	דַּק
tight	mehudak	מְהֻדָּק
totally awesome	chaval al hazman	חֲבָל עַל הַזְּמַן
weak	chalash	חַלָּשׁ
wet	ratuv	רָטוּב
yeshiva style	yeshivati	יְשִׁיבָתִי
young	tza'ir	צָעִיר

Prepositions
Milot Yachas
מִלּוֹת יַחַס

in	betoch	בְּתוֹךְ
with	im	עִם
and	ve...	וְ...
for	bishvil	בִּשְׁבִיל
before	lifnei	לִפְנֵי
after	achrei	אַחֲרֵי

on	al	עַל
to	le...	לְ...
next to	al yad	עַל יָד
here	kan	כָּאן
there	sham	שָׁם
close	karov	קָרוֹב
far	rachok	רָחוֹק
between	bein	בֵּין
until	ad	עַד
over	me'al	מֵעַל
under	mitachat	מִתַּחַת
up	lema'ala	לְמַעְלָה
down	lemata	לְמַטָּה
around	misaviv	מִסָּבִיב
out	bachutz	בַּחוּץ
behind	me'achorei	מֵאֲחוֹרֵי
on the side	batzad	בַּצַּד
opposite	mul	מוּל

Verbs
Pe'alim
פְּעָלִים

All verbs are written in their present-tense, first person, masculine, singular forms.

allow	marsheh	מַרְשֶׁה
answer	oneh	עוֹנֶה
ask	sho'el	שׁוֹאֵל
bake	ofeh	אוֹפֶה
be silent	shotek	שׁוֹתֵק
believe	ma'amin	מַאֲמִין
bless	mevarech	מְבָרֵךְ
bring	mevi	מֵבִיא
call	koreh	קוֹרֵא
change	meshaneh	מְשַׁנֶּה
clean	menakeh	מְנַקֶּה
close	soger	סוֹגֵר
color	tzove'a	צוֹבֵעַ
come	ba	בָּא

cook	mevashel	מְבַשֵׁל
count	sofer	סוֹפֵר
cover	mechaseh	מְכַסֶּה
crawl	zochel	זוֹחֵל
cry	bocheh	בּוֹכֶה
cut	chotech	חוֹתֵךְ
dance	roked	רוֹקֵד
disturb	mafri'a	מַפְרִיעַ
do	oseh	עוֹשֶׂה
drink	shoteh	שׁוֹתֶה
end	gomer	גּוֹמֵר
escort	melaveh	מְלַוֶּה
exchange	machlif	מַחְלִיף
feel	margish	מַרְגִּישׁ
find	motzeh	מוֹצֵא
fix	metaken	מְתַקֵּן
forget	shoche'ach	שׁוֹכֵחַ
give	noten	נוֹתֵן
guard	shomer	שׁוֹמֵר

hear	shome'a	שׁוֹמֵעַ
help	ozer	עוֹזֵר
hope	mekaveh	מְקַוֶּה
jump	kofetz	קוֹפֵץ
know	yode'a	יוֹדֵעַ
laugh	tzochek	צוֹחֵק
lend	malveh	מַלְוֶה
borrow	loveh	לֹוֶה
lie down	shochev	שׁוֹכֵב
live	chai	חַי
look	mistakel	מִסְתַּכֵּל
lose	me'abed	מְאַבֵּד
open	pote'ach	פּוֹתֵחַ
organize	me'argen	מְאַרְגֵּן
pay	meshalem	מְשַׁלֵּם
play	mesachek	מְשַׂחֵק
pour	shofech	שׁוֹפֵךְ
pray	mitpalel	מִתְפַּלֵּל
receive	mekabel	מְקַבֵּל

recognize	makir	מַכִּיר
remember	zocher	זוֹכֵר
remind	mazkir	מַזְכִּיר
rent	socher	שׂוֹכֵר
rent out	maskir	מַשְׂכִּיר
request	mevakesh	מְבַקֵשׁ
run	ratz	רָץ
run away	bore'ach	בּוֹרֵחַ
save	chosech	חוֹסֵךְ
say	omer	אוֹמֵר
schmooze	mesoche'ach	מְשׂוֹחֵחַ
scream	tzo'ek	צוֹעֵק
search	mechapes	מְחַפֵּשׂ
see	ro'eh	רוֹאֶה
sell	mocher	מוֹכֵר
send	shole'ach	שׁוֹלֵחַ
show	mar'eh	מַרְאֶה
sing	shar	שָׁר
sit	yoshev	יוֹשֵׁב

sketch	metzayer	מְצַיֵּר
take	loke'ach	לוֹקֵחַ
smell	meri'ach	מֵרִיחַ
smile	mechayech	מְחַיֵּךְ
swim	socheh	שׂוֹחֶה
take	loke'ach	לוֹקֵחַ
take a stroll	metayel	מְטַיֵּל
take pride	mitga'eh	מִתְגָּאֶה
tell over (i.e. a story)	mesaper	מְסַפֵּר
thank	modeh	מוֹדֶה
think	choshev	חוֹשֵׁב
throw	zorek	זוֹרֵק
travel	nose'a	נוֹסֵעַ
try	menaseh	מְנַסֶּה
visit	mevaker	מְבַקֵּר
wait	mechakeh	מְחַכֶּה
wash	rochetz	רוֹחֵץ
worry	do'eg	דוֹאֵג
write	kotev	כּוֹתֵב

SECTION THREE:
TALK

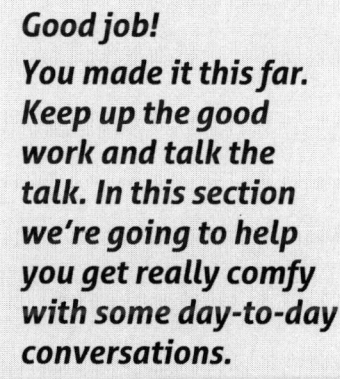

Good job!
You made it this far.
Keep up the good
work and talk the
talk. In this section
we're going to help
you get really comfy
with some day-to-day
conversations.

A New Student
Student Chadash
סְטוּדֶנְט חָדָשׁ

Welcome!	Bruchim haba'im!	בְּרוּכִים הַבָּאִים !
Do you learn here?	Ata lomed po?	אַתָּה לוֹמֵד פֹּה ?
Yes, I am a new student.	Ken ani student chadash.	כֵּן, אֲנִי סְטוּדֶנְט חָדָשׁ.
Where are you from?	Me'eifo ata?	מֵאֵיפֹה אַתָּה ?
I come from Tel Aviv.	Ani ba miTel Aviv.	אֲנִי בָּא מִתֵּל אָבִיב.
What's your name?	Eich korim lecha?	אֵיךְ קוֹרְאִים לְךָ ?
My name is Gadi Elbaz.	Korim li Gadi Elbaz.	קוֹרְאִים לִי גַּדִּי אֶלְבַּז.
Gadi, do you already have friends?	Gadi, yesh lecha kvar chaverim?	גַּדִּי, יֵשׁ לְךָ כְּבָר חֲבֵרִים ?

No, not yet.	Lo, adayin lo.	לֹא, עֲדַיִן לֹא.
I'm Dudu and I'll be your friend. (Don't laugh, in Israel Dudu is a common nickname for David)	Ani Dudu va'ani eh'yeh hechaver shelcha.	אֲנִי דּוּדוּ וַאֲנִי אֶהְיֶה הֶחָבֵר שֶׁלְּךָ.

🎧 MP3**48**

In the Book Store
Bachanut Sefarim
בַּחֲנוּת סְפָרִים

Do you work here?	Ata oved po?	אַתָּה עוֹבֵד פֹּה ?
Yes, How can I help?	Ken, eich efshar la'azor?	כֵּן, אֵיךְ אֶפְשָׁר לַעֲזֹר ?
What do you need?	Ma ata tzarich?	מָה אַתָּה צָרִיךְ ?
I want to buy a phrasebook.	Ani rotzeh liknot sichon.	אֲנִי רוֹצֶה לִקְנוֹת שִׂיחוֹן.

Do you have?	Yesh lachem?	?יֵשׁ לָכֶם
I have many kinds, what kind do you want?	Yesh li harbeh sugim, eizeh ata rotzeh?	יֵשׁ לִי הַרְבֵּה סוּגִים, אֵיזֶה אַתָּה רוֹצֶה?
From English to Hebrew.	Milon Angli-Ivri.	מִילוֹן אַנְגְּלִי-עִבְרִי.
Yeah, I have.	Ken yesh li.	כֵּן, יֵשׁ לִי.
From which publisher?	Me'eizeh motzi la'or?	מֵאֵיזֶה מוֹצִיא לָאוֹר?
It doesn't make a difference.	Lo meshaneh.	לֹא מְשַׁנֶּה.
The best one we have is from Menucha Publishers.	Hachi tov sheyesh lanu, mi'Menucha.	הֲכִי טוֹב שֶׁיֵּשׁ לָנוּ מִמְּנוּחָה.
How much is it?	Kama zeh oleh?	כַּמָּה זֶה עוֹלֶה?
Only 40 shekel.	Rak arba'im shekel.	רַק אַרְבָּעִים שֶׁקֶל.

| What a deal! I'll take two. | Eizeh mivtza! Ekach shnayim. | אֵיזֶה מִבְצָע! אֶקַּח שְׁנַיִם. |

	Sentences/ Expressions for Any Store *Mishpatim/Bituyim Lekol Chanut* מִשְׁפָּטִים/בִּטּוּיִים לְכָל-חֲנוּת	🎧 MP3**49**
Until what time are you open?	Ad matai atem ptuchim?	עַד מָתַי אַתֶּם פְּתוּחִים?
Is there a...?	Yesh...?	יֵשׁ...?
How much does this cost?	Kama zeh oleh?	כַּמָּה זֶה עוֹלֶה?
Is there a cheaper one?	Yesh achad yoter zol?	יֵשׁ אֶחָד יוֹתֵר זוֹל?
Can you order it for me?	Ata yachol lehazmin bishvili?	אַתָּה יָכוֹל לְהַזְמִין בִּשְׁבִילִי?
When will you have it?	Matai yihyeh lachem?	מָתַי יִהְיֶה לָכֶם?

Is it possible to send it the mail?	Efshar lishlo'ach bado'ar?	אֶפְשָׁר לִשְׁלֹחַ בַּדֹּאַר ?
Is it good quality?	Zeh eichuti?	זֶה אֵיכוּתִי ?
Give me a good price.	Ten li mechir tov.	תֵּן לִי מְחִיר טוֹב.
Can you make me a deal?	Ta'aseh li mivtza.	תַּעֲשֶׂה לִי מִבְצָע.
That's no deal at all!	Zeh bichlal lo mivtza!	זֶה בִּכְלָל לֹא מִבְצָע !
Do you have change?	Yesh odef?	יֵשׁ עוֹדֶף ?
Can you give me a receipt?	Efshar kabala?	אֶפְשָׁר קַבָּלָה ?
Give me a bag!	Ten li sakit!	תֵּן לִי שַׂקִּית !
Have you ever heard of customer service?	Pa'am shamata al sherut lakochot?	פַּעַם שָׁמַעְתָּ עַל שֵׁרוּת לָקוּחוֹת ?
I want to speak to the boss.	Ani rotzeh ledaber im ba'al habayit.	אֲנִי רוֹצֶה לְדַבֵּר עִם בַּעַל הַבַּיִת.

Falafel
Falafel
פָלָאפֶל

While in Israel you should make a point of visiting some of its finest falafel joints. I wanna share with you a little method that I learned to help insure that you get a really stuffed pita. You go to the falafel guy and you tell him: "Wow, you know there are so many falafel places out there, but I come here not only for the amazing falafel but mainly for the amazingly large portions."... try it.

You'll have the option to have your falafel in a pita or wrapped in a laffa . I preffer laffa it's kinda like a tortilla, but just betteh.

Also, if you'd like to make the guy happy tell him that it was better than any falafel you've ever had. And if you tell him you want to take a picture with him you'll totally make his day.

On the counter there will be a bottle of amba. It's a mango sauce that really adds a funky flavor to the falafel, first try a little to make sure you like it.

Hi! or Greetings!	Ahalan!	אַהֲלָן !
What do you want?	Ma ata rotzeh?	מָה אַתָּה רוֹצֶה ?
What do you have?	Ma yesh lachem?	מַה יֵּשׁ לָכֶם ?
Falafel in a pita or laffa.	Falafel bepita oh belaffa.	פָלָאפֶל בְּפִיתָה אוֹ בְּלָאפָה.
I want in a laffa.	Ani rotzeh belaffa.	אֲנִי רוֹצֶה בְּלָאפָה.
What do you want inside?	Ma ata rotzeh befnim?	מָה אַתָּה רוֹצֶה בִּפְנִים ?
Give me everything, including fried onions.	Ten li hakol, gam batzal metugan.	תֵּן לִי הַכֹּל, גַּם בָּצָל מְטֻגָּן.
Do you also want hot pepper sauce?	Gam rotzeh charif?	גַּם רוֹצֶה חָרִיף ?
Is it really spicy?	Zeh midai charif?	זֶה מִדַּי חָרִיף ?

Very spicy, we make it here on the spot, it's my grandfather's recipie.	Charif me'od, mechinim et zeh bamakom, mitkon shel saba sheli.	חָרִיף מְאֹד, מְכִינִים אֶת זֶה בַּמָּקוֹם, מַתְכּוֹן שֶׁל סַבָּא שֶׁלִי.
I'm Ashkenazi, not Sefardi, I'll take just a bit.	Ani Ashkenazi, lo Sfaradi, ani ekach rak ketzat.	אֲנִי אַשְׁכְּנַזִּי, לֹא סְפָרַדִּי, אֲנִי אֶקַּח רַק קְצָת.
Hummus, Tehina?	Chumus, tchina?	חוּמוּס, טְחִינָה?
Gimme both.	Shneihem bevakasha.	שְׁנֵיהֶם בְּבַקָּשָׁה.
Wow that looks succulent!	Nir'ah ta'im.	נִרְאָה טָעִים.
Enjoy!	Bete'avon!	בְּתֵאָבוֹן!
Thanks!	Toda!	תּוֹדָה!
Tell your friends.	Tagid lachaverim shelcha.	תַּגִּיד לַחֲבֵרִים שֶׁלְּךָ.

Taxi
Monit
מוֹנִית

Let's take a cab.	Bo nikach bemonit.	בּוֹא נִקַּח מוֹנִית.
I want to go to…	Ani rotzeh (rotza) linso'a leh…	אֲנִי רוֹצֶה (רוֹצָה) לִנְסֹעַ לְ...
Approximately how much will it cost to travel to…?	Be'erech kama ya'aleh linso'a le…?	בְּעֵרֶךְ כַּמָּה יַעֲלֶה לִנְסֹעַ לְ...?
For tourists we have special price.	Letayarim yesh mechir meyuchad.	לְתַיָּרִים יֵשׁ מְחִיר מְיֻחָד.
How much will it be with the meter?	Kama zeh lefi moneh?	כַּמָּה זֶה לְפִי מוֹנֶה?
How much is it with a flat rate?	Kama beli moneh?	כַּמָּה זֶה בְּלִי מוֹנֶה?

Why are you worried, you are American, you have a lot of money.	Lama ata do'eg, ata Amerika'i yesh licha harbeh kesef.	לָמָּה אַתָּה דּוֹאֵג, אַתָּה אֲמֶרִיקָאִי, יֵשׁ לְךָ הַרְבֵּה כֶּסֶף.
Please turn on the meter.	Moneh bevakasha.	מוֹנֶה בְּבַקָּשָׁה.
I'll get out here.	Ani ered kan.	אֲנִי אֵרֵד כָּאן.
If you need ride to airport you kohl me.(cab driver English)	Im titztarech nisi'a lesdeh te'ufa titkasher elai.	אִם תִּצְטָרֵךְ נְסִיעָה לִשְׂדֵה תְּעוּפָה תִּתְקַשֵּׁר אֵלַי.

🎧MP3 52

Speak Hebrew with the Kids
Daber im Hayeladim Be'ivrit
דַּבֵּר עִם הַיְלָדִים בְּעִבְרִית

Good morning my dear son!	Boker tov yeled chamud sheli!	בֹּקֶר טוֹב יֶלֶד חָמוּד שֶׁלִּי!

Good morning my dear daughter!	Boker tov yalda chamuda sheli!	בֹּקֶר טוֹב יַלְדָּה חֲמוּדָה שֶׁלִּי !
Such a good boy!	Eizeh yeled tov!	אֵיזֶה יֶלֶד טוֹב !
Such a good girl!	Eizeh yalda tova!	אֵיזֶה יַלְדָּה טוֹבָה !
Wash your hands.	Tirchatz yadayim.	תִּרְחַץ יָדַיִם.
It's time to get dressed!	Achsahv zeh zman lehitlabesh!	עַכְשָׁו זֶה זְמַן לְהִתְלַבֵּשׁ !
Come here!	Bo lepo!	בּוֹא לְפֹה !
Are you ready?	Muchanim?	מוּכָנִים ?
How was school?	Eich haya bebet sefer?	אֵיךְ הָיָה בְּבֵית סֵפֶר ?
What did you learn today?	Ma lamadta (lamad't) hayom?	מַה לָמַדְתָּ (לָמַדְתְּ) הַיּוֹם ?
Do you want to eat?	Rotzeh (rotza) le'echol?	רוֹצֶה (רוֹצָה) לֶאֱכֹל ?

What do you want to eat?	Ma ata rotzeh (at rotza) le'echol?	מָה אַתָּה רוֹצֶה (אַתְּ רוֹצָה) לֶאֱכֹל ?
Do you want a piece?	Ata rotzeh (At rotza) chaticha?	אַתָּה רוֹצֶה (אַתְּ רוֹצָה) חֲתִיכָה ?
Who do you want to play with?	Im mi ata rotzeh (at rotzah) lesachek?	עִם מִי אַתָּה רוֹצֶה (אַתְּ רוֹצָה) לְשַׂחֵק ?
Play nicely!	Tisachaku yafeh!	תְּשַׂחֲקוּ יָפֶה !
Have a little patience!	Ketzat savlanut!	קְצָת סַבְלָנוּת !
Good night sweety!	Laila tov chamudi!	לַיְלָה טוֹב חָמוּדִי !
Sweet dreams! (lit. golden dreams)	Chalomot paz!	חֲלוֹמוֹת פָּז !
You're the best boy in the whole world!	Ata hayeled hachi tov bichol ha'olam!	אַתָּה הַיֶּלֶד הֲכִי טוֹב בְּכָל-הָעוֹלָם !

You're the best girl in the whole world!	At hayalda hachi tova bichol ha'olam!	אַתְּ הַיַּלְדָּה הֲכִי טוֹבָה בְּכָל־הָעוֹלָם !

DID YOU KNOW THAT... THE NEKUDOT, THE VOWEL SYSTEM OF DOTS AND LINES, ARE NOT PART OF THE ORIGINAL HEBREW? THE SYSTEM WAS CREATED BY THE MASORETES OF TIBERIAS IN THE SECOND HALF OF THE FIRST MILLENNIUM CE. NOWADAYS THEY'RE USUALLY FOUND IN KIDS BOOKS OR RELIGIOUS BOOKS AND OF COURSE IN THE EASY-SHMEEZY GUIDE TO HEBREW.

Many folks quiver when they think about grammar, but I know that since you made it this far you'll be able to handle it. It's really not that crazy....Have a peek.

Word Order

In Hebrew, just as in English the subject comes before the verb. If the sentence includes an object the order will be subject-verb-object.

Yossi drives.	Yossi noheg.	יוֹסִי נוֹהֵג.
Albert likes science.	Albert ohev mada.	אַלְבֶּרְט אוֹהֵב מַדָּע.

Articles

The definite article "the" in Hebrew is *ha*. The article *ha* can precede nouns and adjectives.

the bus	**ha**'otobus	הָאוֹטוֹבּוּס
the tasty falafel	**ha**falafel **ha**ta'im	הַפָלַאפֶל הַטָּעִים

When the definite article *ha* is preceded by the preposition *le* ("to" or "for") or the preposition *be* ("at" or "in"), they're consolidated and turn into *la* ("to the" or "for the") and *ba* ("at the" or "in the").

What bus goes to the Kotel?	Eizeh kav nose'a **la**kotel?	אֵיזֶה קַו נוֹסֵעַ לַכֹּתֶל?
I bought this for the trip.	Kaniti et zeh **la**tiyul.	קָנִיתִי אֶת זֶה לַטִּיּוּל.
They don't have it at the store.	Ein et zeh **ba**chanut.	אֵין אֶת זֶה בַּחֲנוּת.
It's in the old city.	Zeh **Ba**'Ir Ha'atika.	זֶה בָּעִיר הָעַתִּיקָה.

Hebrew does not have the indefinite articles "a" and "an", they're indicated however by the absence of the *ha* in front of the word.

| He eats a shwarma. | Hu ochel shwarma. | הוּא אוֹכֵל שַׁוַוארְמָה. |
| That's an elephant! | Zeh pil! | זֶה פִּיל! |

Prepositions

Hebrew uses three main prepositions that unlike in English when they are used they're attached to the beginning of the word. They are *le/la* ("to" or "for"), *be/ba* ("in" or "with") and *mi/me* ("from").

The present is for Shira.	Hamatana **le**Shira.	הַמַּתָּנָה לְשִׁירָה.
How do you get to Ashdod?	Eich magi'im **le**Ashdod?	אֵיךְ מַגִּיעִים לְאַשְׁדּוֹד ?
She is in the house.	Hi **ba**bayit.	הִיא בַּבַּיִת.
I like falafel in a pita.	Ani ohev falafel **be**pita.	אֲנִי אוֹהֵב פָלָאפֶל בְּפִיתָה.
I'm from Detroit.	Ani **me**Detorit.	אֲנִי מְדֶטְרוֹיְט.
Where are ya'll from?	**Me**'eifo atem?	מֵאֵיפֹה אַתֶּם ?

VERBS

Present Tense

The present tense is similar to English but it covers both "I speak" and "I am speaking". There are singular and plural forms in the present tense for both masculine and feminine. Suffixes are added for most of the pronouns.

I dance (m)	Ani roked	אֲנִי רוֹקֵד
I dance (f)	Ani Roked**et**	אֲנִי רוֹקֶדֶת
you dance (m)	ata roked	אַתָּה רוֹקֵד
you dance (f)	at roked**et**	אַתְּ רוֹקֶדֶת
he dances	hu roked	הוּא רוֹקֵד
she dances	hi roked**et**	הִיא רוֹקֶדֶת
we dance (m)	anachnu rokd**im**	אֲנַחְנוּ רוֹקְדִים
we dance (f)	anachnu rokd**ot**	אֲנַחְנוּ רוֹקְדוֹת
you dance (m,pl)	atem rokd**im**	אַתֶּם רוֹקְדִים
you dance (f,pl)	aten rokd**ot**	אַתֶּן רוֹקְדוֹת

| they dance (m) | hem rokd**im** | הֵם רוֹקְדִים |
| they dance (f) | hen rokd**ot** | הֵן רוֹקְדוֹת |

Past Tense

Just as in present tense, past tense takes on verb endings that will change for the different pronouns. Now here's the thing- the form of the verb in the past tense includes the subject. Thus *halachti* (I went) is a complete sentence including the subject and verb. Here is the break down *halach+ti* (went + I). In truth you could say *ani halachti* and it would be grammatically correct but it just kinda' redundant. Check it out!

I told	Ani sipar**ti**	אֲנִי סִפַּרְתִּי
you told (m)	ata sipar**ta**	אַתָּה סִפַּרְתָּ
you told (f)	at sipar**t**	אַתְּ סִפַּרְתְּ
he told	hu siper	הוּא סִפֵּר
she told	hi sipr**a**	הִיא סִפְּרָה
we told	anachnu sipar**nu**	אֲנַחְנוּ סִפַּרְנוּ
you told (m,pl)	atem sipar**tem**	אַתֶּם סִפַּרְתֶּם
you told (f,pl)	aten sipar**ten**	אַתֶּן סִפַּרְתֶּן

they told (m)	hem sipru	הֵם סִפְּרוּ
they told (f)	hen sipru	הֵן סִפְּרוּ

Future Tense

The verb conjugation in the future tense is similar
to the past tense in that it contains two elements, a
subject and verb. This is done by adding a pronoun
prefix (and sometimes also a suffix) to the future
tense verb stem. Sometimes one will just say
adaber (I will speak) instead of saying Ani + adaber.

I will speak	Ani **a**daber	אֲנִי אֲדַבֵּר
you (m) will speak	ata **te**daber	אַתָּה תְּדַבֵּר
you (f) will speak	at **te**dabri	אַתְּ תְּדַבְּרִי
he will speak	hu **ye**daber	הוּא יְדַבֵּר
she will speak	hi **te**daber	הִיא תְּדַבֵּר
we will speak	anachnu **ne**daber	אֲנַחְנוּ נְדַבֵּר
you (m,pl) will speak	atem **te**dabru	אַתֶּם תְּדַבְּרוּ

you (f,pl) will speak	aten **te**dab**ru**	אַתֶּן תְּדַבְּרוּ
they (m) will speak	hem **ye**dab**ru**	הֵם יְדַבְּרוּ
they (f) will speak	hen **ye**dab**ru**	הֵן יְדַבְּרוּ

DID YOU KNOW THAT... EVEN THOUGH HEBREW WAS NOT USED AS A SPOKEN LANGUAGE FOR HUNDREDS OF YEARS. IT WAS ALWAYS USED AS A WRITTEN LANGUAGE BY TORAH SCHOLARS?

Negatives

The word *lo* meaning no/not is commonly used to negate a sentence. *Lo* can negate a noun, an adjective or a verb.

She isn't a doctor	Hi lo rof'a.	הִיא לֹא רוֹפְאָה.
It's not nice.	Zeh lo yafeh.	זֶה לֹא יָפֶה.
They aren't working now.	Hem lo ovdim achshav.	הֵם לֹא עוֹבְדִים עַכְשָׁו.

Another commonly used form of negation is *ein* meaning there is/are not.

No problem.	Ein be'aya.	אֵין בְּעָיָה.
There's no time.	Ein zman.	אֵין זְמַן.
There isn't enough.	Ein maspik.	אֵין מַסְפִּיק.

SECTION FIVE:
COOL STUFF

This is the section that I call "Cool Stuff" simply because appendix sounds too academic. It's kinda' like a crash course in Israeli culture. Enjoy the songs, jokes and of course the Easy-Shmeezy Guide to bargaining in Israel.

Corny Jokes and Riddles
Bedichot Keresh Vechidot
בְּדִיחוֹת קֶרֶשׁ וְחִידוֹת

What does the Eskimo write in his diary? Today it was cold:	Ma eskimoy kotev bayoman shelo? Hayom haya kar.	מָה אֶסְקִימוֹאִי כּוֹתֵב בַּיוֹמָן שֶׁלוֹ? הַיוֹם הָיָה קַר.
What question should you not ask in the antique store? What's new?	Ma hashe'ela shelo sho'alim bachanut atikot? Ma chadash?	מָה הַשְּׁאֵלָה שֶׁלֹּא שׁוֹאֲלִים בַּחֲנוּת עַתִּיקוֹת? מָה חָדָשׁ.
What did one wall say to the other? Let's meet in the corner.	Ma amar kir echad lakir hasheni? Nipagesh bapina.	מָה אָמַר קִיר אֶחָד לַקִּיר הַשֵּׁנִי? נִפָּגֵשׁ בַּפִּנָּה.

What's the connection between an air conditioner and a computer? They both work slowly when you open windows.	Ma meshutaf lemazgan umachshev? Shneihem ovdim le'at keshepotchim chalonot.	מַה מְשֻׁתָּף לַמַּזְגָּן וּמַחְשֵׁב? שְׁנֵיהֶם עוֹבְדִים לְאַט כְּשֶׁפּוֹתְחִים חַלּוֹנוֹת.
How many psychologists does it take to change a light bulb? One, but the light bulb has to really want it.	Kama p'sichologim tzarich kedei lehachlif nura? Echad, aval tzarich shehanura be'emet yirtzeh.	כַּמָּה פְּסִיכוֹלוֹגִים צָרִיךְ כְּדֵי לְהַחְלִיף נוּרָה? אֶחָד אֲבָל צָרִיךְ שֶׁהַנּוּרָה בֶּאֱמֶת תִּרְצֶה.
What has feathers but can not fly? A feather pillow.	Lemi yesh notzot aval hi lo yechola la'uf? Karit puch.	לְמִי יֵשׁ נוֹצוֹת אֲבָל הִיא לֹא יְכוֹלָה לָעוּף? כָּרִית פּוּךְ.

Why does Mamma Kangaroo hate the rainy days? Because the kids play inside.	Lama ima kengeru son'et yamim geshumim? Ki hayeladim mesachkim bifnim.	לָמָּה אִמָּא קֶנְגְּרוּ שׂוֹנֵאת יָמִים גְּשׁוּמִים? כִּי הַיְלָדִים מְשַׂחֲקִים בִּפְנִים.
What goes around the world, but stays in the corner? A stamp.	Ma mistovev ba'olam aval nish'ar bapina? Bul.	מַה מִסְתּוֹבֵב בָּעוֹלָם אֲבָל נִשְׁאָר בַּפִּנָּה? בּוּל.
What is black when you get it, red when you use it, and white when you're done with it? A coal.	Ma shachor keshemekablim oto, adom keshemish-tamshim bo, velavan keshegomrim ito? Pecham.	מַה שָׁחוֹר כְּשֶׁמְּקַבְּלִים אוֹתוֹ, אָדוֹם כְּשֶׁמִּשְׁתַּמְּשִׁים בּוֹ, וְלָבָן כְּשֶׁגּוֹמְרִים אִתּוֹ? פֶּחָם.

What can be put in a box that will make it weigh less? Holes.	Ma efshar lasim bekufsa sheyorid et mishkala? Chorim.	מָה אֶפְשָׁר לָשִׂים בְּקֻפְסָה שֶׁיּוֹרִיד אֶת מִשְׁקָלָהּ? חוֹרִים.
What is filled with holes but continues to hold water? A sponge.	Ma maleh chorim aval mamshich lehachzik mayim? Sefog.	מָה מָלֵא חוֹרִים אֲבָל מַמְשִׁיךְ לְהַחְזִיק מַיִם? סְפוֹג.
When does Chanuka come before Sukkot? When looking in an encyclopedia.	Matai ba Chanuka lifnei Sukot? Keshemechpasim ba'entziklo-ped'ya.	מָתַי בָּא חֲנֻכָּה לִפְנֵי סֻכּוֹת? כְּשֶׁמְּחַפְּשִׂים בָּאֶנְצִיקְלוֹפֶּדְיָה.
What can fill up a room but doesn't take up any space? Light.	Ma yachol lemaleh cheder aval lo tofes makom? Or.	מָה יָכוֹל לְמַלֵּא חֶדֶר אֲבָל לֹא תּוֹפֵס מָקוֹם? אוֹר.

What can you catch but can't throw? A cold.	Ma efshar litpos aval ee efshar lizrok? Hitztanenut.	מָה אֶפְשָׁר לִתְפֹּס אֲבָל אִי אֶפְשָׁר לִזְרֹק? הַצְּטַנְּנוּת.
Why is the math book sad? Because it's filled with problems.	Lama sefer matematika atzuv? Biglal shehu maleh be'ayot.	לָמָה סֵפֶר מָתֶמָטִיקָה עָצוּב? בִּגְלַל שֶׁהוּא מָלֵא בְּעָיוֹת.
What has four legs but can't walk? A table.	Lema yesh arba raglayim aval lo yachol lalechet? Shulchan.	לְמָה יֵשׁ אַרְבַּע רַגְלַיִם אֲבָל לֹא יָכוֹל לָלֶכֶת? שֻׁלְחָן.
Why did the child study in an airplane? He wanted to receive a higher education.	Lama hayeled lamad ba'aviron? Hu ratza lekabel chinuch gavoha.	לָמָה הַיֶּלֶד לָמַד בָּאֲוִירוֹן? הוּא רָצָה לְקַבֵּל חִנּוּךְ גָּבוֹהַּ.

| When do you stop at green and go at red? When eating watermelon. | Matai otzrim bayarok umitkadmim ba'adom? Keshe'ochlim avati'ach. | מָתַי עוֹצְרִים בְּיָרוֹק וּמִתְקַדְּמִים בְּאָדוֹם ? כְּשֶׁאוֹכְלִים אֲבַטִּיחַ. |
| Which treatment does a plant undergo at the dentist? A root canal. | Eizeh tipul over tzemach etzel rofeh shinayim? Tipul shoresh. | אֵיזֶה טִפּוּל עוֹבֵר צֶמַח אֵצֶל רוֹפֵא שִׁנַּיִם ? טִפּוּל שֹׁרֶשׁ. |

DID YOU EVER HEAR OF THE 99/1 PRINCIPLE? IT SUGGESTS THAT 99% OF HEBREW CONVERSATION USES ONLY 1% OF THE HEBREW LANGUAGE. THAT'S PRETTY COOL. THAT MEANS YOU DON'T HAVE TO KNOW THE WHOLE DICTIONARY TO START SPEAKING. THERE IS A BOOK THAT TEACHES HEBREW BASED ON THE PRINCIPLE. THE BOOK IS CALLED THE EASY–SHMEEZY GUIDE TO HEBREW.

Tongue Twisters
Shover Shinayim
שׁוֹבֵר שִׁנַיִם

Gad fishes tickling fish on the riverbank.	Gad dag dagim medagdegim bagada.	גַּד דָּג דָּגִים מְדַגְדְּגִים בַּגָּדָה.
Who stopped him from mumbling words?	Mi mana mimenu milemalmel milim?	מִי מָנַע מִמֶּנּוּ מִלְמַלְמֵל מִלִּים?
Sarah sings a happy song, a happy song sings Sarah.	Sara shara shir sameach, shir sameach shara Sara.	שָׂרָה שָׁרָה שִׁיר שָׂמֵחַ, שִׁיר שָׂמֵחַ שָׂרָה שָׂרָה.
A snake bit a snake that bit a snake.	Nachash nashach nachash shenashach nachash.	נָחָשׁ נָשַׁךְ נָחָשׁ שֶׁנָּשַׁךְ נָחָשׁ.
Sheep washed laundry.	Kivsa kivsa kevisa.	כִּבְשָׂה כִּבְּסָה כְּבִיסָה.

A Bisl Yiddish too!

🎧MP3**55**

The founding fathers of Israel all spoke Yiddish as their mother tongue. Due to this, Hebrew is filled with Yiddish words, proverbs and linguistics. When Hebrew lacked a certain word or expression they didn't hesitate to use a bisl Yiddish. The following is just a small list:

old stuff	alteh zachen	אַלְטֶע זַאכְן
suspenders	shlaikes	שְׁלַייקֶס
a big fat lie	blof	בְּלוֹף
burp	greps	גְרֶעפְּס
jitney/one who does odd jobs	chaper	חַאפֶּר
big shot/busy guy	macher	מַאכֶער
annoying fellow	nudnik	נוּדְנִיק
unfortunate fellow	nebach	נֶעבַּאךְ
little details	pitshifkes	פִּיצְ׳יפְקֶס
looser/sucker	frayer	פְרַאייֶר
snitch/informer	shtinker	שְׁטִינְקֶר

junk	shmattes	שְׁמַאטֶעס
unkempt dresser	shlomper	שְׁלוֹמְפֶּר
clumsy fellow	shlumi'el	שְׁלוֹמִיאֵל

A Lil' Arabic

🎧 MP3 56

Here is a small sample of the many Arabic words that made it into Hebrew. Naturally, as you'd probably assume, there are many Hebrew words that also snuck their way into Arabic.

Get a move on!/Let's go!	Yaala!	יַאלְלָה
like/as	yaani	יַעְנִי
fun	kef	כֵּיף
cool	sababa	סַבַּבָּה
awesome	achla	אַחְלָה
mistake	fashla	פַשְׁלָה
an embarrassing situation	fadicha	פָדִיחָה
Wow!	Walla!	וַואלְלָה!
Howdy!	Ahalahn!	אַהֲלָן

Hey dude/ bro (lit. my beloved)	chabibi	חַבִּיבִי
haircut given at age three	chalakeh	חַלָאקֶה
sloppy job	chafif	חֲפִיף
barbeque	mangal	מַנְגַּל
falafel	falafel	פָלָאפֶל
couscous	kuskus	קוּסְקוּס
hummus	chumus	חוּמוּס

Kim'at Angleet- Almost English 🎧 MP3 57

Here is a small sample of the hundreds of Hebrew words that come from English… simply *magniv* (magnificent).

technology	technologiya	טֶכְנוֹלוֹגְיָה
cellphone	selulari	סֶלוּלָרִי
email	meyl	מֵייל
pleats	pants	פֶּנְטְס
relevant	relevanti	רֶלַוַנְטִי

realistic	reali	רֵאָלִי
actual	actuali	אַקְטוּאָלִי
dramatic	dramati	דְרָמָטִי
principle	prensip	פְּרֶנְצִיפּ
hi-tech	haitech	הַייטֶק
feedback	fidbak	פִידְבֶּק
back axle	bak axle	בֶּק אֶקְסֶל
front axle	bak axle kidmi	בֶּק אֶקְסֶל קִדְמִי
shock	shok	שׁוֹק
shopping	shopping	שׁוֹפִּינג
finishing touches	finishim	פִינִישִׁים
freezer	freezer	פְרִיזֶר
refridgerator	fridgider	פְרִידְגִ׳ידֶר
optimistic	optimi	אוֹפְּטִימִי
pessimistic	pesimi	פֶּסִימִי
coffee	kafe	קָפֶה
tea	tei	תֶּה
barbeque	bar-b-kyu	בַּרְבִּיקְיוּ
vulgar	volgari	ווּלְגָרִי

internet	internet	אִינְטֶרְנֶט
bonus	bonus	בּוֹנוּס
jeans	jins	ג׳ינְס
business	biznis	בִּיזְנֶס
boss	bos	בּוֹס
blender	blender	בְּלֶנְדֶר
lobby	lobi	לוֹבִּי
tissue	tishyu	טִישׁוּ
baby sitter	beibi siter	בֵּייבִּי סִיטֶר
jungle	jungel	ג׳וּנְגֶל
video	vidyo	וִידֵאוֹ
lipstick	lipstik	לִיפְּסְטִיק
deal	dil	דִיל
duplex	dupleks	דוּפְּלֶקְס
model	model	מוֹדֶל
tip	tip	טִיפּ
plus	plus	פְּלוּס
campaign	kampein	קַמְפֵּיין
startup	startap	סְטַרְטַאפּ

to patrol	lefatrel	לְפַטְרֵל
to fax	lefakses	לְפַקְסֵס
to make a telephone call	letalfen	לְטַלְפֵן
to discuss	ledaskes	לְדַסְקֵס
to acclimate	lehitaklem	לְהִתְאַקְלֵם

Salam Aleikum!

🎧 MP3**58**

Arabic is Israel's second most widely spoken language. No matter where you are in Israel you are not far from an Arab community. I decided to put this section in the book just in case you end up in an Arab village. Keep in mind that most Arabs in Israel speak Hebrew, however in the west bank many Arabs don't speak much Hebrew at all.

Please.	Min fadlach.
Thank you.	Shukran.
You're welcome.	Afwan.
Yes.	Ai-wa.
No.	La.

I don't understand.	Mish fahim.
Do you speak English?	Tech-ki Englizi?
Hello.	A-halan.
Goodbye.	Ma-ah-salameh.
Good morning.	Sabach al-chir.
Good evening/night.	Masa-al-chir.
Which bus goes to...?	Aya bas yaruch ala...?
right	yemineh
left	sh'mal.
straight	du-ree

Ha-Ha-Ha---HACHOOOOO!

In Israel not only do the people speak a different language but so do the birds, dogs and sneezes... that's right the sneezes.

Instead of "cock-a-doodle-doo" the roosters say "koo-koo-rikoo".

Instead of "tweet-tweet" the birds say "tzif tzif".

Instead of "woof-woof" the dogs say "haw-haw".

Instead of "knock-knock" the sound your fist makes hitting the door is "tuk-tuk".

Instead of "haa-choo!", when you sneeze you'll say "up-chee!".

Instead of "umm" when you're unsure of something...you'll say "emm".

Instead of "ouch!" when you stub your toe you'll say "ahyaa!".

Instead of "oh-no!" upon hearing bad news you'll say "oohf!".

Instead of "psst-psst!" to get someones attention you'll say "tsz-tsz" {besides being the attention grabbing sound, the "tsz-tsz" is also used to scare away stray cats near public dumpsters}.

Bargaining

As a general rule most mom n' pop kind of stores, meaning not supermarkets and franchise stores, will be able to bargain. If you walk in there with your fanny pack and oversized camera they'll know you're a rich tourist and the odds will be against you. But if you ditch the fanny pack and camera here are some lines that should help you make a deal. The key to success in bargaining is your confidence; basically try to hold your poker face and poker tone of voice... (easier said than done). Also, you'll have much better luck in the Arab shuk (market) simply because they'll first quote you an astronomically high price, and also because they feel the pain of a lost customer more than an Israeli. Meaning that the Israeli would rather forfeit the sale for his pride and say "okay, don't buy here I have other customers" whereas the Arab merchant will really strive to make a sale even if he'll only make a few shekels.

| That looks nice, how much is that? | Zeh nira yafeh, kama zeh oleh? | זֶה נִרְאָה יָפֶה כַּמָּה זֶה עוֹלֶה? |
| Ten shekel. | Eser shekel. | עֶשֶׂר שֶׁקֶל. |

Whoa! No thanks	Wai! Lo toda.	וַי! לֹא תּוֹדָה.
What? It's very good price!	Ma? Zeh mechir metzuyan!	מַה? זֶה מְחִיר מְצֻיָּן!
I'll tell you, I thought it'd be much less, like half of that.	Ani agid lecha, chashavti sheyihyeh harbeh yoter zol, kachatzi mizeh.	אֲנִי אַגִּיד לְךָ, חָשַׁבְתִּי שֶׁיִּהְיֶה הַרְבֵּה יוֹתֵר זוֹל, כַּחֲצִי מִזֶּה.
No way, with the price I quoted I actually lose money.	Lo lo, im hamechir she'amarti ani davka mafsid.	לֹא לֹא, עִם הַמְּחִיר שֶׁאֲנִי אָמַרְתִּי אֲנִי דַּוְקָא מַפְסִיד.
The truth is that I don't really have that much room in my suitcase to take it home.	Ha'emet hi she'be'etzem ein li makom bamizvada lakachat et zeh habaita.	הָאֱמֶת הִיא שֶׁבְּעֶצֶם אֵין לִי מָקוֹם בַּמִּזְוָדָה שֶׁלִּי לָקַחַת אֶת זֶה הַבַּיְתָה.
Thanks anyway.	Todah bechol zot.	תּוֹדָה בְּכָל־זֹאת.

Come back for a second, okay I'll give it to you for five shekel.	Bo rega, bseder ani etein lecha bechamesh shekel.	בֹּא רֶגַע, בְּסֵדֶר אֲנִי אֶתֵּן לְךָ בְּחָמֵשׁ שֶׁקֶל.
You should know that I've never given a price like this before.	Teda she'af pa'am lo natati mechir kazeh.	תֵּדַע שֶׁאַף פַּעַם לֹא נָתַתִּי מְחִיר כָּזֶה.

DID YOU KNOW THAT OVER 7 MILLION PEOPLE WORLDWIDE SPEAK HEBREW? IN THE USA ALONE, THERE ARE OVER 200,000 NATIVE SPEAKERS AS WELL AS MANY MORE NON-NATIVE SPEAKERS.

Dreidel Song
Sevivon
סְבִיבוֹן

Spinning top, spin spin spin
Chanukah is a great holiday
A Happy Holiday for everyone,
A great miracle happened here,
A Happy Holiday for everyone.

| Sevivon, sov sov sov,
Chanukah hu chag tov
Chanukah hu chag tov
Sevivon, sov sov sov. | סְבִיבוֹן, סוֹב סוֹב סוֹב,
חֲנֻכָּה הוּא חַג טוֹב
חֲנֻכָּה הוּא חַג טוֹב
סְבִיבוֹן, סוֹב סוֹב סוֹב. |
| Sov na sov, ko va cho,
Nes gadol haya po,
Nes gadol haya po
Sevivon, sov sov sov. | סוֹב נָא סוֹב, כֹּה וָכֹה,
נֵס גָּדוֹל הָיָה פֹּה,
נֵס גָּדוֹל הָיָה פֹּה
סְבִיבוֹן, סוֹב סוֹב סוֹב. |

Purim
Chag Purim
חַג פּוּרִים

🎧MP3**61**

Purim time Purim time
A big festival for the Jewish people

Masks, noisemakers
songs and dances.

Let's make noise - "rash rash rash"
Let's make noise - "rash rash rash"
Let's make noise - "rash rash rash"
With noisemakers.

Purim time
Purim time
we send gifts to one another

Treats, sweets
and other nice things.

Let's make noise - "rash rash rash"
Let's make noise - "rash rash rash"
Let's make noise - "rash rash rash"
With noisemakers.

Chag Purim Chag Purim	חַג פּוּרִים חַג פּוּרִים
Chag gadol layehudim Masechot, ra'ashanim, shirim verikudim.	חַג גָּדוֹל לַיְהוּדִים מַסֵּכוֹת, רַעֲשָׁנִים, שִׁירִים וְרִקּוּדִים.
Hava narisha - rash, rash, rash, Hava narisha - rash, rash, rash,Hava narisha - rash, rash, rash, Bara'ashanim.	הָבָה נַרְעִישָׁה - רַשׁ, רַשׁ, רַשׁ, הָבָה נַרְעִישָׁה - רַשׁ, רַשׁ, רַשׁ, הָבָה נַרְעִישָׁה - רַשׁ, רַשׁ, רַשׁ, בָּרַעֲשָׁנִים.
Chag Purim Chag Purim	חַג פּוּרִים חַג פּוּרִים
zeh el zeh sholchim manot, Machmadim, mamtakim, Tunifim migdanot.	זֶה אֶל זֶה שׁוֹלְחִים מָנוֹת, מַחְמַדִּים, מַמְתַּקִּים, תּוֹפִינִים מִגְדָנוֹת.
Hava narisha - rash, rash, rash, Hava narisha - rash, rash, rash, Hava narisha - rash, rash, rash, Bara'ashanim.	הָבָה נַרְעִישָׁה - רַשׁ, רַשׁ, רַשׁ, הָבָה נַרְעִישָׁה - רַשׁ, רַשׁ, רַשׁ, הָבָה נַרְעִישָׁה - רַשׁ, רַשׁ, רַשׁ, בָּרַעֲשָׁנִים.

Tu Bishvat is Here!
Tu Bishvat Higi'a
ט״ו בִּשְׁבָט הִגִּיעַ

🎧 MP3 62

The almond tree is blooming
and the golden sun is shining,
birds atop each roof
announce the arrival of the festival.

Tu bishvat has arrived
the festival of trees.
Tu bishvat has arrived
the festival of trees.

The land is crying out
the time of planting has arrived
each person shall take a tree
we'll stride out with spades.

Tu bishvat has arrived...

The sun is shining
and it's very hot today
I hope the weather
stays bright.

Hashkediyah porachat veshemesh paz zorachat, tziporim merosh kol gag mevasrot et bo hachag.	הַשְּׁקֵדִיָּה פּוֹרַחַת וְשֶׁמֶשׁ פָּז זוֹרַחַת, צִפּוֹרִים מֵרֹאשׁ כָּל-גַּג מְבַשְּׂרוֹת אֶת בּוֹא הֶחָג.
T"u bishvat higi'a chag la'ilanot. T"u bishvat higi'a chag la'ilanot. Ha'aretz meshava'at higi'a et lata'at kol echad yikach lo etz be'atim nitzeh chotzetz.	ט״וּ בִּשְׁבָט הִגִּיעַ חַג לָאִילָנוֹת. ט״וּ בִּשְׁבָט הִגִּיעַ חַג לָאִילָנוֹת. הָאָרֶץ מְשַׁוַּעַת הִגִּיעַ עֵת לָטַעַת כָּל-אֶחָד יִקַּח לוֹ עֵץ בְּאֵתִים נֵצֵא חוֹצֵץ.
T"u bish'vat higi'a…	ט״וּ בִּשְׁבָט הִגִּיעַ…
Hashemesh zorachat vecham meod hayom. ani mekava mezeg ha'avir sheyisha'er bahir.	הַשֶּׁמֶשׁ זוֹרַחַת וְחַם מְאֹד הַיּוֹם. אֲנִי מְקַוֶּה מֶזֶג הָאֲוִיר שֶׁיִּשָּׁאֵר בָּהִיר.

Today is Your Birthday
Hayom Yom Huledet
הַיּוֹם יוֹם הֻלֶּדֶת

🎧MP3 63

Today is a b-day,
today is a b-day,
today is a b-day,
for_____.
He/she's got a joyous holiday,
A set of flowers blooms for him/her,
today is a b-day,
for_____.

Hayom yom huledet	הַיּוֹם יוֹם הֻלֶּדֶת
hayom yom huledet	הַיּוֹם יוֹם הֻלֶּדֶת
hayom yom huledet	הַיּוֹם יוֹם הֻלֶּדֶת
le_____.	לְ_____
Chag lo/la same'ach	חַג לוֹ/לָהּ שָׂמֵחַ
vezer lo/la pore'ach	וְזֵר לוֹ/לָהּ פּוֹרֵחַ
hayom yom huledet	הַיּוֹם יוֹם הֻלֶּדֶת
le_____.	לְ_____

CONGRATULATIONS!
You've finished The
Easy-Shmeezy Guide
to Hebrew. It probably
feels cool to be able to
speak the language of
Israel. Perhaps you've
opened up doors for
yourself, either socially
or academically. These
resources will help you
continue growing as a
Hebrew speaker.

www.EasyShmeezy.com

The Easy-Shmeezy Foundation was established with a focus on bringing the beauty of Jewish culture to Jews worldwide.

Make sure to check out **www.Easyshmeezy.com** to find the best ways to continue your Hebrew studies. You might decide that you want to learn with a private teacher or join an online group class. You should also get yourself the Easy-Shmeezy Hebrew mp3s. In any case, check it out.

Recommended Books:

- Hebrew/English Dictionary by Shimon Zilberman.

- The Guide to Lashon Hakodesh by Nachman Marcuson. (This workbook is great for mastering Biblical Hebrew. I have personally taught courses based on this guide.)

- If you've decided it's time to move on to the *Mammeh Loshn* treat yourself to The Easy-Shmeezy Guide to Yiddish.

Free Stuff:

- Check out www.hebrew-jokes.com and www.in-hebrew.co.il for hours of Hebrew fun.

- www.DoItInHebrew.com is an extensive Online Hebrew Dictionary, Translation and Transliteration engine. Anyone can quickly learn to type in Hebrew using their Phonetic Hebrew Keyboard and then view dictionary definitions and translations from around the web in a single click – all for free. Paid subscribers receive translations complete with vowels (menukad) and transliterations for nearly any word or phrase and may even hear it played back in Hebrew audio. Turn on "cursive" mode to view your translations in Hebrew cursive script. They also offer past, present, future and command form verb conjugations for over 1,500 Hebrew verb roots (shoreshim).

- If you've been so inspired by this book that you've decided you wanna move to Israel go to www.nbn.org.il. That's Nefesh B'Nefesh. They'll walk you through the whole aliyah process, and if you tell them

I sent you they might even give you some cash to help out with the move.

- Take a peek at www.kolhalashon.com where you can download thousands of Torah classes in Hebrew on all sorts of topics.

The best way to work on your Hebrew is by using a **H.H.P. — Hebrew Helper Pal**. Get one of these, it's totally worth it. An H.P.P. is a friend or relative who you can call and ask your questions. It's great if they speak Hebrew on a native level, but the most important thing is that they speak a higher level than you.

T.T.Y. — Talk To Yourself. That's right — talk to yourself and have conversations in Hebrew. You'll see where you get stuck and what kind of words you need help with. Write those words down and seek help from your H.H.P. (It is recommended to have the T.T.Y. conversations in private. I have one student however, who actually does them on the bus or while shopping. When he told me this I thought it was absurd, but really it is not so crazy. He said he just wears a Bluetooth headpiece and people think he's talkin' on the phone.)

And remember, whenever you learn a new word make sure you write it down.

In order to help you build your vocabulary, I've added this section for you to write down words or phrases that you'd like to learn. For example: Let's say you wonder how to say "Where can I get a *falafel* around here?" Just write it down and the next time you speak to your H.H.P. (Hebrew Helper Pal) you can ask him for the translation — that's truly Easy-Shmeezy!

How do you say?	? אֵיךְ אוֹמְרִים
Where can I get a *falafel* around here?	אֵיפֹה אֲנִי יָכוֹל לִקְנוֹת פַאלַאפֶל בָּאֵזוֹר ?
I want to be a zookeeper when I grow up.	

DICTIONARY

a couple of years \ kama shanim \ כַּמָּה שָׁנִים

a half of an hour \ chatzi sha'a \ חֲצִי שָׁעָה

a little \ ketzat \ קְצָת

a little time \ ketzat zman \ קְצָת זְמַן

a long time \ harbeh zman \ הַרְבֵּה זְמַן

a lot \ harbeh \ הַרְבֵּה

a quarter of an hour \ reva sha'a \ רֶבַע שָׁעָה

adult pass \ kartisiya regila \ כַּרְטִיסִיָּה רְגִילָה

after \ achrei \ אַחֲרֵי

afternoon \ achrei hatzaharayim \ אַחֲרֵי הַצָּהֳרַיִם

again \ od hapa'am \ עוֹד הַפַּעַם

air \ avir \ אֲוִיר

airplane \ matos \ מָטוֹס

all \ hakol \ הַכֹּל

allow \ marsheh \ מַרְשֶׁה

almonds \ shkedim \ שְׁקֵדִים

also \ gam \ גַּם

and \ ve... \ ו

answer \ oneh \ עוֹנֶה

apple \ tapu'ach \ תַּפּוּחַ

apricot \ mishmesh \ מִשְׁמֵשׁ

Are you voting? \ ata matzbi'a? \ אַתָּה מַצְבִּיעַ?

arm \ zro'a \ זְרוֹעַ

around \ misaviv \ מִסָּבִיב

ask \ sho'el \ שׁוֹאֵל

at night \ balaila \ בַּלַּיְלָה

at the traffic light \ baramzor \ בָּרַמְזוֹר

attic \ boydem \ בּוֹיְדֶעם

aunt \ doda \ דּוֹדָה

awesome \ madhim \ מַדְהִים

back \ gav \ גַּב

back door \ delet achorit \ דֶּלֶת אֲחוֹרִית

bad \ ra \ רַע

bake \ ofeh \ אוֹפֶה

balcony \ mirpeset \ מִרְפֶּסֶת

banana \ banana \ בָּנָנָה

basement \ martef \ מַרְתֵּף

bathroom \ sherutim \ שֵׁרוּתִים

Be quiet! \ Sheket! \ שֶׁקֶט!

be silent \ shotek \ שׁוֹתֵק

beach \ chof \ חוֹף

beans \ sha'u'it \ שְׁעוּעִית

bear \ dov \ דֹּב

beard \ zakan \ זָקָן

bed \ mita \ מִטָּה

bedroom \ chadar sheina \ חֲדַר שֵׁנָה

beer \ bira \ בִּירָה

before \ lifnei \ לִפְנֵי

before noon \ lifnei hatzaharayim \ לִפְנֵי הַצָּהֳרַיִם

behind \ me'achorei \ מֵאֲחוֹרֵי

believe \ ma'amin \ מַאֲמִין

belly \ beten \ בֶּטֶן

belt \ chagora \ חֲגוֹרָה

bench \ safsal \ סַפְסָל

berry \ tut \ תּוּת

between \ bein \ בֵּין

bicycle \ ofanayim \ אוֹפַנַיִם

big \ gadol \ גָּדוֹל

bird \ tzipor \ צִפּוֹר

black \ shachor \ שָׁחוֹר

blanket \ smicha \ שְׂמִיכָה

bless \ mevarech \ מְבָרֵךְ

blood \ dam \ דָּם

blue \ kachol \ כָּחֹל

body \ guf \ גּוּף

bone \ etzem \ עֶצֶם

book shelf \ aron sfarim \ אֲרוֹן סְפָרִים

books \ sfarim \ סְפָרִים

boots \ magafayim \ מַגָּפַיִם

borrow \ loveh \ לוֹוֶה

boy \ yeled \ יֶלֶד

branches \ anafim \ עֲנָפִים

bread \ lechem \ לֶחֶם

breakfast \ aruchat boker \ אֲרוּחַת בֹּקֶר

bridge \ gesher \ גֶּשֶׁר

bring \ mevi \ מֵבִיא

broken \ shavur \ שָׁבוּר

brother \ ach \ אָח

brother-in-law \ gis \ גִּיס

brown \ chum \ חוּם

building \ binyan \ בִּנְיָן

bus \ otobus \ אוֹטוֹבּוּס

bus card \ rav kav \ רַב קַו

bus pass \ kartisiya \ כַּרְטִיסִיָּה

bus stop \ tachanat otobus \ תַּחֲנַת אוֹטוֹבּוּס

butter \ chema \ חֶמְאָה

by the way \ derech agav \ דֶּרֶךְ אַגַב

Bye! \ Bai! \ בַּיי!

CEO \ menahel (minahelet) \ מְנַהֵל (מְנַהֶלֶת)

cabbage \ kruv \ כְּרוּב

cake \ uga \ עוּגָה

call \ koreh \ קוֹרֵא

Call a doctor \ K'ra lerofeh \ קְרָא לְרוֹפֵא

Call me tomorrow \ Titkasher elai machar \ תִּתְקַשֵּׁר אֵלַי מָחָר

camel \ gamal \ גָּמָל

Can I get there by foot? \ Efshar lalechet lesham baregel? \ אֶפְשָׁר לָלֶכֶת לְשָׁם בָּרֶגֶל?

Can I speak with Yossi? \ Efshar ledaber im Yossi? \ אֶפְשָׁר לְדַבֵּר עִם יוֹסִי?

Can't be \ Lo yitachen \ לֹא יִתָּכֵן

car \ oto/rechev \ אוֹטוֹ/ רֶכֶב

carrot \ gezer \ גֶּזֶר

cat \ chatula \ חֲתוּלָה

ceiling \ tikra \ תִּקְרָה

celery \ seleri \ סֶלֶרִי

cell phone \ telefon nayad/pelefon \ טֶלֶפוֹן נַיָּד/פֶּלֶאפוֹן

central bus station \ tachana merkazit \ תַּחֲנָה מֶרְכָּזִית

certainly \ bevadai \ בְּוַדַּאי

chair \ kiseh \ כִּסֵּא

change \ meshaneh \ מְשַׁנֶּה

cheap \ zol \ זוֹל

cheek \ lechi \ לֶחִי

cheese \ gvina \ גְּבִינָה

cherry \ duvdevan \ דּוּבְדְּבָן

chicken \ ohf \ עוֹף

children \ yeladim \ יְלָדִים

clean (adj) \ naki \ נָקִי

clean (verb) \ menakeh \ מְנַקֶה

close (adj) \ karov \ קָרוֹב

close (verb) \ soger \ סוֹגֵר

Close the window \ S'gor et hachalon \ סְגוֹר אֶת הַחַלוֹן

closed \ sagur \ סָגוּר

closet \ aron \ אָרוֹן

clouds \ ananim \ עֲנָנִים

cloudy \ me'unan \ מְעֻנָן

coalition \ ko'alitzi'a \ קוֹאֲלִיצְיָה

coat \ me'il \ מְעִיל

coffee \ kafeh \ קָפֶה

cola \ kola \ קוֹלָה

cold \ kar \ קַר

cold drink \ shtiya kara \ שְׁתִיָה קָרָה

color \ tzove'a \ צוֹבֵעַ

come \ ba \ בָּא

come here \ bo lepo \ בּוֹא לְפֹה

complete \ shalem \ שָׁלֵם

computer \ machshev \ מַחְשֵׁב

cook \ mevashel \ מְבַשֵׁל

cookie \ ugiya \ עֻגִיָה

cool \ karir \ קָרִיר

correct \ nachon \ נָכוֹן

couch \ sapa \ סַפָּה

count \ sofer \ סוֹפֵר

counter \ shayesh \ שַׁיִשׁ

cousin \ ben dod \ בֶּן דוֹד

cover \ mechaseh \ מְכַסֶה

cow \ para \ פָּרָה

crackers \ krekerim \ קְרֵקֵרִים

crawl \ zochel \ זוֹחֵל

cream of the crop \ salta veshamna \ סָלְתָּה וּשְׁמֵנָה

crosswalk \ ma'avar chatzaya \ מַעֲבַר חֲצָיָה

cry \ bocheh \ בּוֹכֶה

cucumber \ melafefon \ מְלָפְפוֹן

cut \ chotech \ חוֹתֵךְ

dance \ roked \ רוֹקֵד

dark \ keheh \ כֵּהֶה

date \ tamar \ תָּמָר

daughter \ bat \ בַּת

daughter-in-law \ kala \ כַּלָה

day \ yom \ יוֹם

deer \ tzvi \ צְבִי

dentist \ rofeh (rof'at) shinayim \ רוֹפֵא (רוֹפְאַת) שִׁנַיִם

difficult \ kasheh \ קָשֶׁה

dinner \ aruchat erev \ אֲרוּחַת עֶרֶב

dirty \ meluchlach \ מְלֻכְלָךְ

disturb \ mafri'a \ מַפְרִיעַ

do \ oseh \ עוֹשֶׂה

doctor \ rofeh (rof'a) \ רוֹפֵא (רוֹפְאָה)

dog \ kelev \ כֶּלֶב

don't bother me \ al tafri'a li \ אַל תַּפְרִיעַ לִי

don't exaggerate \ lo lehagzim \ לֹא לְהַגְזִים!

donkey \ chamor \ חֲמוֹר

door \ delet \ דֶּלֶת

down \ lemata \ לְמַטָּה

drawer \ megera \ מְגֵרָה

dress \ simla \ שִׂמְלָה

drink \ shoteh \ שׁוֹתֶה

driver's license \ risheyon nehiga \ רִשְׁיוֹן נְהִיגָה

dry \ yavesh \ יָבֵשׁ

duck \ barvaz \ בַּרְוָז

ear \ ozen \ אֹזֶן

early \ mukdam \ מֻקְדָם

earthquake \ re'idat adama \ רְעִידַת אֲדָמָה

east \ mizrach \ מִזְרָח

easy/easy-shmeezy \ kal \ קַל

eggs \ beitzim \ בֵּיצִים

election \ bechirot \ בְּחִירוֹת

electric outlet \ sheka \ שֶׁקַע

elephant \ pil \ פִּיל

email \ meil \ מֵייל

empty \ reik \ רֵיק

end \ gomer \ גּוֹמֵר

engineer \ mehandes (mehandeset) \ מְהַנְדֵּס (מְהַנְדֶּסֶת)

enough \ maspik \ מַסְפִּיק

escort \ melaveh \ מְלַוֶּה

everyday \ kol yom \ כָּל-יוֹם

exactly \ bediyuk \ בְּדִיּוּק

excellent \ p'tzatza \ פְּצָצָה

exchange \ machlif \ מַחְלִיף

excuse me \ slicha \ סְלִיחָה

expensive \ yakar \ יָקָר

eye \ ayin \ עַיִן

eyebrows \ gabot \ גַּבּוֹת

face \ panim \ פָּנִים

falafel \ falafel \ פָלָאפֶל

fall (season) \ stav \ סְתָיו

fan \ me'avrer \ מְאַוְרֵר

far \ rachok \ רָחוֹק

fast \ maher \ מַהֵר

father \ aba \ אַבָּא

father-in-law \ choten/shver \ חוֹתֵן/ שְׁוֶּר

faucet \ berez \ בֶּרֶז

feel \ margish \ מַרְגִּישׁ

field \ sadeh \ שָׂדֶה

fig \ te'ena \ תְּאֵנָה

find \ motzeh \ מוֹצֵא

fine \ beseder \ בְּסֵדֶר

finger \ etzba \ אֶצְבַּע

fish \ dag \ דָּג

fix \ metaken \ מְתַקֵּן

flood \ mabul \ מַבּוּל

floor \ ritzpa \ רִצְפָּה

flowers \ prachim \ פְּרָחִים

foggy \ arafel \ עֲרָפֶל

foot \ regel \ רֶגֶל

for \ bishvil \ בִּשְׁבִיל

forecast \ tachazit \ תַּחֲזִית

forehead \ metzach \ מֵצַח

forget \ shoche'ach \ שׁוֹכֵחַ

fork \ mazleg \ מַזְלֵג

fox \ shu'al \ שׁוּעָל

Friday \ Yom Shishi \ יוֹם שִׁשִּׁי

friends \ chaverim \ חֲבֵרִים

frog \ tzfardei'a \ צְפַרְדֵּעַ

from A to Z \ me'alef ad tav \ מֵאָלֶף עַד תָּיו

front door \ delet kidmit \ דֶּלֶת קִדְמִית

frying pan \ machvat \ מַחֲבַת

full \ maleh \ מָלֵא

furniture \ rihut \ רִהוּט

garbage can \ pach \ פַּח

garden \ gina \ גִּנָּה

garlic \ shum \ שׁוּם

gate \ gader \ גָּדֵר

girl \ yalda \ יַלְדָּה

give \ noten \ נוֹתֵן

Give me a glass of \ Ten li kos… \ תֶּן לִי כּוֹס…

glasses \ mishkafayim \ מִשְׁקָפַיִם

gloves \ k'fafot \ כְּפָפוֹת

Go all the way to the end \ Yashar yashar

ad hasof \ יָשָׁר יָשָׁר עַד הַסּוֹף

Go away \ Lech mikan \ לֵךְ מִכָּאן

gold \ zahav \ זָהָב

good \ tov \ טוֹב

Good afternoon! \ Tzaharayim tovim! \ צָהֳרַיִם טוֹבִים!

Good day! \ Yom tov! \ יוֹם טוֹב!

Good evening! \ Erev tov! \ עֶרֶב טוֹב!

Good luck! \ Behatzlacha! \ בְּהַצְלָחָה!

Good month! \ Chodesh tov! \ חֹדֶשׁ טוֹב!

Good morning! \ Boker tov! \ בֹּקֶר טוֹב!

Good night! \ Laila tov! \ לַיְלָה טוֹב!

Good week! \ Shavu'a tov! \ שָׁבוּעַ טוֹב!

goodbye \ yala bai \ יָאללָה בַּיי

goose \ avaz \ אַוָּז

government \ memshala \ מֶמְשָׁלָה

grandchild \ neched \ נֶכֶד

grandfather \ saba \ סַבָּא

grandmother \ savta \ סַבְתָּא

grapefruit \ eshkolit \ אֶשְׁכּוֹלִית

grapes \ anavim \ עֲנָבִים

grass \ deshe \ דֶּשֶׁא

gray \ afor \ אָפֹר

great \ metzuyan \ מְצֻיָּן

great grandfather \ saba raba \ סַבָּא רַבָּא

great grandmother \ savta raba \ סַבְתָּא רַבָּה

great-grandchild \ nin \ נִין

green \ yarok \ יָרֹק

guard \ shomer \ שׁוֹמֵר

hair \ se'ar \ שֵׂעָר

hand \ yad \ יָד

hard \ kasheh \ קָשֶׁה

hat \ kova \ כּוֹבַע

Have a good trip! \ Nesiya tova! \ נְסִיעָה

טוֹבָה!

Have a look \ Tistakel (Tistakli) \ תִּסְתַּכֵּל (תִּסְתַּכְּלִי)

Have a seat \ Shev (Sh'vi) \ שֵׁב (שְׁבִי)

he \ hu \ הוּא

He can't speak now \ Hu lo yachol ledaber achshav \ הוּא לֹא יָכוֹל לְדַבֵּר עַכְשָׁו

He cut me off! \ Hu akaf oti! \ הוּא עָקַף אוֹתִי!

He eats a lot of... \ Hu ochel harbeh \ הוּא אֹכֵל הַרְבֵּה

He's got a screw loose \ Nafal lo boreg \ נָפַל לוֹ בֹּרֶג

head \ rosh \ רֹאשׁ

hear \ shome'a \ שׁוֹמֵעַ

heart \ lev \ לֵב

Hello! (only used when answering phone) \ Allo! \ הָלוֹ!

Hello/Goodbye! \ Shalom! \ שָׁלוֹם!

help (verb) \ ozer \ עוֹזֵר

hers \ shela \ שֶׁלָּהּ

here \ po/kan \ פֹּה/כָּאן

highway \ kvish mahir \ כְּבִישׁ מָהִיר

his \ shelo \ שֶׁלּוֹ

homepage \ daf habayit \ דַּף הַבַּיִת

hope \ mekaveh \ מְקַוֶּה

horrible \ al hapanim \ עַל הַפָּנִים

horse \ sus \ סוּס

hot \ cham \ חַם

hot drink \ shtiya chama \ שְׁתִיָּה חַמָּה

hour \ sha'a \ שָׁעָה

house/home \ bayit \ בַּיִת

houses \ batim \ בָּתִּים

How are things? \ Ma ha'inyanim? \ מָה הָעִנְיָנִים?

How are you feeling? \ Eich ata margish (at margisha) \ אֵיךְ אַתָּה מַרְגִּישׁ (אַתְּ מַרְגִּישָׁה)?

How are you? \ Ma shlomcha (shlomech)? \ מה שלומך (שלומך)?

How do I get to? \ Eich magi'im le…? \ איך מגיעים ל?

How much? \ Kama? \ כמה?

How? \ Eich? \ איך?

How's the weather? \ Eich mezeg ha'avir? \ מה מזג האויר?

humid \ lach \ לח

hummus \ chumus \ חומוס

husband \ baal \ בעל

I \ Ani \ אני

I am a \ Ani \ אני

I am angry \ Ani ko'es (ko'eset) \ אני כועס (כועסת)

I am confused \ Ani mivulbal (mivulbelet) \ אני מבולבל (מבולבלת)

I am embarrassed \ Ani mitbayesh (mitbayeshet) \ אני מתבייש (מתביישת)

I am excited \ Ani metragesh (mitrageshet) \ אני מתרגש (מתרגשת)

I am happy \ Ani same'ach (smecha) \ אני שמח (שמחה)

I am insulted \ Ne'elavti \ נעלבתי

I am not pleased \ Ani lo merutzeh (merutza) \ אני לא מרוצה (מרוצה)

I am pleased \ Ani merutzeh (merutza) \ אני מרוצה (מרוצה)

I am sad \ Ani atzuv (atzuva) \ אני עצוב (עצובה)

I am scared \ Ani mefached (mefachedet) \ אני מפחד (מפחדת)

I am tired \ Ani ayeif (ayeifa) \ אני עייף (עיפה)

I am worried \ Ani mud'ag (mud'eget) \ אני מודאג (מודאגת)

I don't feel well \ Ani margish tov (margisha tova) \ אני לא מרגיש טוב (מרגישה)

I don't have any energy \ Ein li ko'ach \ אין לי כח

I don't have any time \ Ein li zman \ אין לי זמן

I don't have \ Ein li \ אין לי

I don't know \ Ani lo yode'a (yoda'at) \ לא יודע (יודעת)

I don't like \ Ani lo ohev (ohevet)… \ אני לא אוהב (אוהבת)

I don't remember \ Ani lo zocher (zocheret) \ אני לא זוכר (זוכרת)

I don't think so \ Ani choshev (choshevet) shelo \ אני חושב (חושבת) שלא

I don't understand \ Ani lo mevin (mevina) \ אני לא מבין (מבינה)

I forgot \ Shachachti \ שכחתי

I hate \ Ani soneh (sona'at)… \ אני שונא (שונאת)

I have energy \ Yesh li ko'ach \ יש לי כח

I have \ Yesh li \ יש לי

I know already \ Ani kvar yode'a (yoda'at) \ אני כבר יודע (יודעת)

I know \ Ani yode'a (yoda'at) \ אני יודע (יודעת)

I like to eat…… \ Ani ohev (ohevet) le'echol… \ אני אוהב (אוהבת) לאכול

I like \ Ani ohev (ohevet)… \ אני אוהב (אוהבת)

I make a lot of money \ Ani marvi'ach (marvicha) harbeh kesef \ אני מרויח (מרויחה) הרבה כסף

I regret \ Ani mitcharet (mitcharetet) \ אני מתחרט (מתחרטת)

I want to buy \ Ani rotzeh (rotza) liknot \ אני רוצה (רוצה) לקנות

I want to eat borekas \ Ani rotzeh (rotza) le'echol burekas \ אני רוצה (רוצה) לאכול בורקס

I want to speak Hebrew \ Ani rotzeh (rotza) ledaber Ivrit \ אני רוצה (רוצה) לדבר עברית

I wear my _____ \ Ani lovesh (loveshet) et ha_____ sheli אֲנִי לוֹבֵשׁ\ (לוֹבֶשֶׁת) אֶת ה_____שֶׁלִּי

I work in a big office \ Ani oved (ovedet) bemisrad gadol \ אֲנִי עוֹבֵד (עוֹבֶדֶת) בְּמִשְׂרָד גָּדוֹל

I'll scratch your back you scratch mine \ Shmor li, eshmor licha \ שְׁמוֹר לִי, אֶשְׁמוֹר לְךָ

I'm fine \ Ani beseder \ אֲנִי בְּסֵדֶר

I'm hungry \ Ani ra'ev (re'eva) \ אֲנִי רָעֵב (רְעֵבָה)

I'm learning Hebrew \ Ani lomed (lomedet) Ivrit \ אֲנִי לוֹמֵד (לוֹמֶדֶת) עִבְרִית

I'm now learning to speak \ Achshav ani lomed (lomedet) ledaber \ עַכְשָׁו אֲנִי לוֹמֵד (לוֹמֶדֶת) לְדַבֵּר

I'm thirsty \ Ani tzameh (tzme'a) \ אֲנִי צָמֵא (צְמֵאָה)

I'm... \ Ani... \ ...אֲנִי

I've had it \ Nishbar li \ נִשְׁבַּר לִי

important \ chashuv \ חָשׁוּב

in \ be... \ ...בְּ

Inside \ betoch \ בְּתוֹךְ

In Israel it doesn't rain in the summer \ BeYisra'el lo yored geshem bakayitz \ בְּיִשְׂרָאֵל לֹא יוֹרֵד גֶּשֶׁם בַּקַּיִץ

In the evening \ ba'erev \ בָּעֶרֶב

in the morning \ baboker \ בַּבֹּקֶר

In the shuk there many kinds of fruits \ Bashuk yesh harbeh sugei peirot \ בַּשּׁוּק יֵשׁ הַרְבֵּה סוּגֵי פֵּרוֹת

in-laws \ mechutanim \ מְחֻתָּנִים

Indeed?(!) \ Be'emet?(!) \ בֶּאֱמֶת?(!)

interesting \ me'anyen \ מְעַנְיֵן

intersection \ tzomet \ צֹמֶת

In your dreams \ Bachalomot \ בַּחֲלוֹמוֹת

Is it actually easy? \ Zeh be'emet kal? \ זֶה בֶּאֱמֶת קַל?

Is it far from here? \ Zeh rachok mikan? \ זֶה רָחוֹק מִכָּאן?

Is the matter urgent? \ Zeh dachuf? \ זֶה דָּחוּף?

It doesn't make a difference/Never mind \ Lo meshaneh \ לֹא מְשַׁנֶּה

It seems so \ Nireh li sh

eken \ נִרְאֶה לִי שֶׁכֵּן

It's healthy to eat vegetables \ Zeh bari le'echol yerakot \ זֶה בָּרִיא לֶאֱכוֹל יְרָקוֹת

It's not your business \ Zeh lo ha'esek shelcha (shelach) \ זֶה לֹא הָעֵסֶק שֶׁלְּךָ (שֶׁלָּךְ)

It's only talk \ Zeh rak diburim \ זֶה רַק דִּבּוּרִים

It's raining \ Yored geshem \ יוֹרֵד גֶּשֶׁם

It's snowing \ Yored sheleg \ יוֹרֵד שֶׁלֶג

It's storming outside \ So'er bachutz \ סוֹעֵר בַּחוּץ

It's very very good! \ Masheu masheu! \ מַשֶּׁהוּ מַשֶּׁהוּ!

It's... \ Zeh... \ ...זֶה

journalist \ itonai (itona'it) \ עִיתוֹנַאי (עִיתוֹנָאִית)

juice \ mitz \ מִיץ

jump \ kofetz \ קוֹפֵץ

junk-food \ chatifim \ חֲטִיפִים

kettle \ kumkum \ קַמְקוּם

keyboard \ mikledet \ מִקְלֶדֶת

keys \ maftechot \ מַפְתְּחוֹת

kitchen \ mitbach \ מִטְבָּח

knee \ berech \ בֶּרֶךְ

knife \ sakin \ סַכִּין

knit skullcap \ kipa sruga \ כִּפָּה סְרוּגָה

know \ yode'a \ יוֹדֵעַ

kollel guy \ avrech \ אַבְרֵךְ

ladle \ matzeket \ מַצֶּקֶת

lake \ agam \ אֲגַם

land \ eretz \ אֶרֶץ

lane \ netiv \ נָתִיב

laptop \ machshev nayad \ מַחשֵׁב נַיָד

last but not least \ achron achron chaviv \ אַחֲרוֹן אַחֲרוֹן חָבִיב

last year \ hashana she'avra \ הַשָׁנָה שֶׁעָבְרָה

late \ me'uchar \ מְאֻחָר

laugh \ tzochek \ צוֹחֵק

lawyer \ orech (orechet) din \ עוֹרֵךְ (עוֹרֶכֶת) דִין

Leave me alone \ Ta'azov oti \ תַעֲזֹב אוֹתִי

lemon \ limon \ לִימוֹן

lend \ malveh \ מַלוֶה

lie down \ shochev \ שׁוֹכֵב

light (adj) \ bahir \ בָּהִיר

lightning \ barak \ בָּרָק

lights \ te'ura \ תְאוּרָה

link \ kishur \ קִשּׁוּר

lion \ aryeh \ אַרְיֵה

lips \ sfatayim \ שְׂפָתַיִם

liquor \ mashke charif \ מַשׁקֶה חָרִיף

Listen up \ Takshiv (Takshivi) \ תַקשִׁיב (תַקשִׁיבִי)

live \ chai \ חַי

living room \ salon \ סָלוֹן

long \ aroch \ אָרֹךְ

look \ mistakel \ מִסְתַכֵּל

loose \ rafui \ רָפוּי

lose \ me'abed \ מְאַבֵּד

low \ namuch \ נָמוּךְ

lunch \ aruchat tzaharayim \ אֲרוּחַת צָהֳרַיִם

Make yourself at home \ Targish (Targishi) babayit \ תַרְגִישׁ (תַרְגִישִׁי) בַּבַּיִת

man \ gever \ גֶבֶר

many years \ harbeh shanim \ הַרְבֵּה שָׁנִים

maybe \ ulai \ אוּלַי

mayor \ rosh ha'ir \ רֹאשׁ הָעִיר

meat \ basar \ בָּשָׂר

melon \ melon \ מֶלוֹן

member of parliament \ chaver keneset \ חָבֵר כְּנֶסֶת

milk \ chalav \ חָלָב

mine \ sheli \ שֶׁלִי

minister \ sar \ שַׂר

minute \ daka \ דַקָה

moment \ rega \ רֶגַע

Monday \ Yom Sheni \ יוֹם שֵׁנִי

money \ kesef \ כֶּסֶף

monkey \ kof \ קוֹף

month \ chodesh \ חֹדֶשׁ

moon \ yare'ach \ יָרֵחַ

mother \ ima \ אִמָא

mother-in-law \ chamot \ חָמוֹת

motorcycle \ ofano'a \ אוֹפַנוֹעַ

mountain \ har \ הַר

mouse \ achbar \ עַכְבָּר

moustache \ safam \ שָׂפָם

mouth \ pe \ פֶּה

mud \ botz \ בּוֹץ

My favorite color is blue \ Hatzeva she'ani hachi ohev hu kachol \ הַצֶבַע שֶׁאֲנִי הֲכִי אוֹהֵב הוּא כָּחֹל

My hand hurts \ Ko'ev li hayad \ כּוֹאֵב לִי הַיָד

My son loves the zoo \ Haben sheli ohev et gan hachayot \ הַבֵּן שֶׁלִי אוֹהֵב אֶת גַן הַחַיוֹת

My vote doesn't make a difference \ Hakol sheli lo mashpi'a \ הַקוֹל שֶׁלִי לֹא מַשׁפִּיעַ

nail \ tziporen \ צִפֹּרֶן

napkin \ mapiyon \ מַפִּיוֹן

natural spring \ ma'eyan \ מַעְיָן

neck \ tzavar \ צַוָאר

nephew \ achyan \ אַחיָן

new \ chadash \ חָדָשׁ

new driver \ nehag chadash \ נֶהָג חָדָשׁ

newspaper \ iton \ עִתּוֹן

next to \ al yad \ עַל יָד

next year \ hashana haba'a \ הַשָּׁנָה הַבָּאָה

nice \ yafe/na'im \ יָפֶה/נָעִים

niece \ achyanit \ אַחְיָנִית

no \ lo \ לֹא

No difference \ Ein hevdel \ אֵין הֶבְדֵּל

No doubt \ Ein safek \ אֵין סָפֵק

No thanks \ Lo toda \ לֹא תוֹדָה

No way José \ Ein matzav \ אֵין מַצָּב

nonsense \ shtuyot \ שְׁטוּיוֹת

noodles \ itri'ot \ אִטְרִיּוֹת

noon \ tzaharayim \ צָהֳרַיִם

normal \ normali \ נוֹרְמָלִי

north \ tsafon \ צָפוֹן

nose \ af \ אַף

not good \ lo tov \ לֹא טוֹב

not like that \ lo kacha \ לֹא כָּכָה

not yet \ adayin lo \ עֲדַיִן לֹא

notebook \ machberet \ מַחְבֶּרֶת

nothin' at all \ klum \ כְּלוּם

now \ achshav \ עַכְשָׁו

nuts \ egozim \ אֱגוֹזִים

Oh no! \ Oy-va-voy! \ אוֹי וַאֲבוֹי!

Okay \ Beseder \ בְּסֵדֶר

old \ yashan \ יָשָׁן

olive \ zayit \ זַיִת

on \ al \ עַל

on the side \ batzad \ בַּצַּד

onion \ batzal \ בָּצָל

only \ rak \ רַק

open (adj) \ patu'ach \ פָּתוּחַ

open (verb) \ pote'ach \ פּוֹתֵחַ

opposite \ mul \ מוּל

orange (fruit) \ tapuz \ תַּפּוּז

orange (color) \ katom \ כָּתֹם

organize \ me'argen \ מְאַרְגֵּן

our \ shelanu \ שֶׁלָּנוּ

out \ bachutz \ בַּחוּץ

oven \ tanur \ תַּנּוּר

over \ me'al \ מֵעַל

pants \ michnasayim \ מִכְנָסַיִם

paper \ niyar \ נְיָר

parents \ horim \ הוֹרִים

parliament \ knesset \ כְּנֶסֶת

password \ sisma \ סִסְמָא

pay \ meshalem \ מְשַׁלֵּם

peach \ afarsek \ אֲפַרְסֵק

pear \ agas \ אַגָּס

pen \ et \ עֵט

pencil \ iparon \ עִפָּרוֹן

pepper \ pilpel \ פִּלְפֵּל

pillow \ karit \ כָּרִית

pink \ varod \ וָרֹד

plate \ tzalachat \ צַלַּחַת

play \ mesachek \ מְשַׂחֵק

please \ bevakasha \ בְּבַקָּשָׁה

pleasent \ na'im \ נָעִים

plum \ shezif \ שְׁזִיף

pocket \ kis \ כִּיס

police \ mishtara \ מִשְׁטָרָה

pomegranate \ rimon \ רִמּוֹן

poor \ ani \ עָנִי

pot \ sir \ סִיר

potato \ tapu'ach adama \ תַּפּוּחַ אֲדָמָה

pound sign (phone) \ sulamit \ סוּלָמִית

English \ Transliteration	Hebrew
pour \ shofech	שׁוֹפֵךְ
pray \ mitpalel	מִתְפַּלֵל
president \ nasi	נָשִׂיא
pretzels \ beigalach	בֵּייגֶלַךְ
prime minister \ rosh hamemshala	רֹאשׁ הַמֶּמְשָׁלָה
program \ tochna	תּוֹכְנָה
propaganda \ ta'aluma	תַּעֲמוּלָה
purple \ segol	סָגוֹל
purse \ tik	תִּיק
rabbi \ rav	רַב
radish \ tznon	צְנוֹן
rainbow \ keshet	קֶשֶׁת
receipt \ kabala	קַבָּלָה
receive \ mekabel	מְקַבֵּל
recognize \ makir	מַכִּיר
red \ adom	אָדֹם
regards \ dash	ד"שׁ
remember \ zochor	זוֹכֵר
remind \ mazkir	מַזְכִּיר
rent \ socher	שׂוֹכֵר
rent out \ maskir	מַשְׂכִּיר
request \ mevakesh	מְבַקֵּשׁ
rice \ orez	אוֹרֶז
rich \ ashir	עָשִׁיר
ring \ tziltzul	צִלְצוּל
river \ nahar	נָהָר
road \ kvish	כְּבִישׁ
roll (n.) \ lachmaniya	לַחְמָנִיָּה
roof \ gag	גַּג
room \ cheder	חֶדֶר
roots \ sharashim	שָׁרָשִׁים
round trip \ haloch vachazor	הָלוֹךְ וַחֲזוֹר
run \ ratz	רָץ

English \ Transliteration	Hebrew
run away \ bore'ach	בּוֹרֵחַ
salad \ salat	סָלָט
salary \ maskoret	מַשְׂכֹּרֶת
salt \ melach	מֶלַח
salt shaker \ milchiya	מִלְחִיָּה
same thing \ oto davar	אוֹתוֹ דָּבָר
sand \ chol	חוֹל
sandwich \ karich/sendvitsh	כָּרִיךְ/סֶנְדְוִויץ'
Saturday \ Shabbat	שַׁבָּת
save \ chosech	חוֹסֵךְ
say \ omer	אוֹמֵר
say it again \ Tagid Shuv	תַּגִיד שׁוּב
scarf \ tza'if	צָעִיף
schmooze \ mesoche'ach	מְשׂוֹחֵחַ
school \ beit sefer	בֵּית סֵפֶר
scientist \ mad'an (ma'adanit)	מַדְעָן (מַדְעָנִית)
scream \ tzo'ek	צוֹעֵק
screen \ masach	מָסָךְ
sea \ yam	יָם
search \ mechapes	מְחַפֵּשׂ
search engine \ mano'a chipus	מָנוֹעַ חִפּוּשׂ
second \ shniya	שְׁנִיָּה
secretary \ mazkir (mazkira)	מַזְכִּיר (מַזְכִּירָה)
see \ ro'eh	רוֹאֶה
See you later! \ Lehitra'ot!	לְהִתְרָאוֹת!
sell \ mocher	מוֹכֵר
send \ shole'ach	שׁוֹלֵחַ
she \ hi	הִיא
she loves to eat \ Hi ohevet le'echol	הִיא אוֹהֶבֶת לֶאֱכֹל
sheep \ keves	כֶּבֶשׂ
shirt \ chultza	חֻלְצָה
shoes \ na'alayim	נַעֲלַיִם

short \ katzar \ קָצָר
shoulder \ katef \ כָּתֵף
show \ mar'eh \ מַרְאֶה
sidewalk \ midracha \ מִדְרָכָה
silver \ kesef \ כֶּסֶף
sing \ shar \ שָׁר
sink \ kiyor \ כִּיוֹר
sister \ achot \ אָחוֹת
sister-in-law \ gisa \ גִּיסָה
sit \ yoshev \ יוֹשֵׁב
sketch \ metzayer \ מְצַיֵּר
skullcap \ kipa \ כִּפָּה
sky \ shamayim \ שָׁמַיִם
slow \ le'at \ לְאַט
small \ katan \ קָטָן
smell \ meri'ach \ מֵרִיחַ
smile \ mechayech \ מְחַיֵּךְ
snake \ nachash \ נָחָשׁ
so so \ Kacha kacha \ כָּכָה כָּכָה
socks \ garbayim \ גַּרְבַּיִם
soft \ rach \ רַךְ
son \ ben \ בֵּן
son-in-law \ chatan \ חָתָן
soup \ marak \ מָרָק
south \ darom \ דָּרוֹם
speak a little slower \ Tedaber (Tedabri) ketzat yoter le'at \ (תְּדַבֵּר (תְּדַבְּרִי) קְצָת יוֹתֵר לְאַט
speed bump \ pas he'ata \ פַּס הַאֲטָה
spoon \ kapit \ כַּפִּית
spring \ aviv \ אָבִיב
sprouts \ nevatim \ נְבָטִים
squash \ dla'at \ דְּלַעַת
stairs \ madregot \ מַדְרֵגוֹת

star key (telephone) \ kochavit \ כּוֹכָבִית
stars \ kochavim \ כּוֹכָבִים
stones \ avanim \ אֲבָנִים
stop light \ ramzor \ רַמְזוֹר
stores \ chanuyot \ חֲנֻיּוֹת
storm \ se'ara \ סְעָרָה
stove \ kirayim \ כִּירַיִם
straight ahead \ Yashar \ יָשָׁר
strange \ muzar \ מוּזָר
street \ rechov \ רְחוֹב
strong \ chazak \ חָזָק
student \ student (studentit) \ סְטוּדֶנְט (סְטוּדֶנְטִית)
sugar \ sukar \ סֻכָּר
suit \ chalifa \ חֲלִיפָה
summer \ kayitz \ קַיִץ
sun \ shemesh \ שֶׁמֶשׁ
Sunday \ Yom Rishon \ יוֹם רִאשׁוֹן
sunflower seeds \ gar'inim \ גַּרְעִינִים
sunny \ bahir \ בָּהִיר
sweetheart \ neshama \ נְשָׁמָה
swim \ socheh \ שׂוֹחֶה
synagogue \ beit keneset \ בֵּית כְּנֶסֶת
table \ shulchan \ שֻׁלְחָן
take \ loke'ach \ לוֹקֵחַ
take a right \ Yamina \ יָמִינָה
take a left \ Smola \ שְׂמֹאלָה
take a stroll \ metayel \ מְטַיֵּל
take pride \ mitga'eh \ מִתְגָּאֶה
tall \ gavoha \ גָּבוֹהַּ
tasty \ ta'im \ טָעִים
tea \ tei \ תֵּה
teacher \ moreh (mora) \ (מוֹרָה)
technology \ technologiya \ טֶכְנוֹלוֹגְיָה

teeth \ shinayim \ שִׁנַּיִם

tell over (i.e. a story) \ mesaper \ מְסַפֵּר

text message \ sms \ אֶס אֶם אֶס

thank \ modeh \ מוֹדֶה

thank G-d, great \ baruch Hashem, metzuyan \ בָּרוּךְ הַשֵּׁם, מְצֻיָּן

thank you very much \ toda raba \ תּוֹדָה רַבָּה

thank you \ toda \ תּוֹדָה

that's how it goes \ kacha zeh holech \ כָּכָה זֶה הוֹלֵךְ

that's it \ zehu zeh \ זֶהוּ זֶה

that's not cool/that's not okay \ zeh lo beseder \ זֶה לֹא בְּסֵדֶר

the best! \ hachi tov! \ הֲכִי טוֹב!

the cherry on the cream \ haduvdevan shebakatzefet \ הַדֻּבְדְּבָן שֶׁבַּקֶּצֶפֶת

the day after tomorrow \ machratayim \ מָחֳרָתַיִם

the family is coming for shabbos \ hamishpacha magi'a leshabat \ הַמִּשְׁפָּחָה מַגִּיעָה לְשַׁבָּת

the grass is green \ hadesheh yarok \ הַדֶּשֶׁא יָרֹק

the straw that broke the camel's back \ hakash sheshavar et gav hagamal \ הַקַּשׁ שֶׁשָּׁבַר אֶת גַּב הַגָּמָל

the way it should be \ kimo shetzarich \ כְּמוֹ שֶׁצָּרִיךְ

the weather is... \ mezeg ha'avir hu... \ מֶזֶג הָאֲוִיר הוּא...

their (f) \ shelhen \ שֶׁלָּהֶן

their (m) \ shelhem \ שֶׁלָּהֶם

there \ sham \ שָׁם

they (m) \ hem \ הֵם

they (f) \ hen \ הֵן

thick \ aveh \ עָבֶה

thigh \ yarech \ יָרֵךְ

thin \ dak \ דַּק

think \ choshev \ חוֹשֵׁב

this \ zeh \ זֶה

this is blue \ zeh kachol \ זֶה כָּחֹל

this year \ hashana hazot \ הַשָּׁנָה הַזֹּאת

throw \ zorek \ זוֹרֵק

thunder \ ra'am \ רַעַם

thursday \ yom chamishi \ יוֹם חֲמִישִׁי

tie (n.) \ aniva \ עֲנִיבָה

tiger \ namer \ נָמֵר

tight \ mehudak \ מְהֻדָּק

time \ zman \ זְמַן

time will tell \ yamim yagidu \ יָמִים יַגִּידוּ

to \ le... \ לְ...

to profit \ leharvi'ach \ לְהַרְוִיחַ

to surf \ liglosh \ לִגְלֹשׁ

today \ hayom \ הַיּוֹם

tomato \ agvaniya \ עַגְבָנִיָּה

tomorrow \ machar \ מָחָר

tongue \ lashon \ לָשׁוֹן

tools \ klei avoda \ כְּלֵי עֲבוֹדָה

totally awesome (lit a waste of time) \ chaval al hazman \ חֲבָל עַל הַזְּמַן

towel \ magevet \ מַגֶּבֶת

toys \ mischakim \ מִשְׂחָקִים

travel \ nose'a \ נוֹסֵעַ

tray \ magash \ מַגָּשׁ

tree \ etz \ עֵץ

tree trunk \ geza \ גֶּזַע

truck \ masa'it \ מַשָּׂאִית

truthfully \ be'emet \ בֶּאֱמֶת

try \ menaseh \ מְנַסֶּה

try later \ tenaseh me'uchar yoter \ תְּנַסֶּה מְאֻחָר יוֹתֵר

Tuesday \ Yom Shlishi \ יוֹם שְׁלִישִׁי

tunnel \ minhara \ מִנְהָרָה

turkey \ hodu \ הוֹדוּ

two days ago \ lifnei yomayim \ שִׁלְשׁוֹם

two o'clock \ hasha'a shtayim \ הַשָּׁעָה שְׁתַּיִם

two weeks ago \ lifnei shvu'ayim \ לִפְנֵי שְׁבוּעַיִם

unbelievable \ lo ye'uman \ לֹא יֵאָמֵן

uncle \ dod \ דּוֹד

under \ mitachat \ מִתַּחַת

underwear \ tachtonim \ תַּחְתּוֹנִים

until \ ad \ עַד

unusual \ yotzeh dofen \ יוֹצֵא דֹּפֶן

up \ lema'ala \ לְמַעְלָה

vegetation \ tzmachim \ צְמָחִים

very easy \ kal me'od \ קַל מְאֹד

very nice \ yafeh me'od \ יָפֶה מְאֹד

visit \ mevaker \ מְבַקֵּר

voice mail \ ta hakoli \ תָּא הַקּוֹלִי

vote \ lehatzbi'a \ לְהַצְבִּיעַ

wait \ mechakeh \ מְחַכֶּה

wait a second \ chakeh rega \ חַכֵּה (חַכִּי) רֶגַע

wall \ kir \ קִיר

wallet \ arnak \ אַרְנָק

wash \ rochetz \ רוֹחֵץ

watch \ sha'on yad \ שָׁעוֹן יָד

water \ mayim \ מַיִם

waterfall \ mapal \ מַפָּל

we \ anachnu \ אֲנַחְנוּ

we grew up together \ gadalnu biyachad \ גָּדַלְנוּ בְּיַחַד

we'll be in touch \ nihyeh bekesher \ נִהְיֶה בְּקֶשֶׁר

weak \ chalash \ חַלָּשׁ

website \ atar \ אֲתַר

Wednesday \ Yom Revi'i \ יוֹם רְבִיעִי

week \ shavu'a \ שָׁבוּעַ

weekend \ sof shavu'a \ סוֹף שָׁבוּעַ

west \ ma'arav \ מַעֲרָב

wet \ ratuv \ רָטוֹב

what a ... \ eizeh ... \ אֵיזֶה ...

what a jerk! \ eizeh metoraf! \ אֵיזֶה מְטוֹרָף!

what are you talkin' about?! (this expression means: really?!) \ mah ata omer (at omeret)?! \ מָה אַתָּה אוֹמֵר (אַתְּ אוֹמֶרֶת)?!

what color is this? \ eizeh tzeva zeh? \ אֵיזֶה צֶבַע זֶה?

what do i care? \ ma ichpat li? \ מָה אִכְפַּת לִי?

what do you do for a living? \ ma ata oseh (at osa) bachayim? \ מָה אַתָּה עוֹשֶׂה (אַתְּ עוֹשָׂה) בַּחַיִּים?

what does he want to eat? \ ma hu rotzeh le'echol? \ מָה הוּא רוֹצֶה לֶאֱכֹל?

what happened? \ ma kara? \ מָה קָרָה?

what kinda work do you do? \ bema ata oved (at ovedet)? \ בַּמֶּה אַתָּה עוֹבֵד (אַתְּ עוֹבֶדֶת)?

what? \ ma? \ מָה?

what's doing? \ ma ha'inyanim? \ מָה הָעִנְיָנִים?

what's happening? \ ma koreh? \ מָה קוֹרֶה?

what's new? \ ma chadash? \ מָה חָדָשׁ?

what's up? \ ma nishma? \ מָה נִשְׁמַע?

when? \ matai? \ מָתַי?

where? \ eifo? \ אֵיפֹה?

where're you from? \ me'eifo ata (at)? \ מֵאֵיפֹה אַתָּה (אַתְּ)?

which? \ eizeh? \ אֵיזֶה?

white \ lavan \ לָבָן

who are you voting for? \ lemi ata matzbi'a? \ לְמִי אַתָּה מַצְבִּיעַ?

who is this? \ mi zeh? \ מִי זֶה?

who? \ mi? \ ‏מִי?‏

whoa! \ wai wai! \ ‏וַי וַי!‏

why? \ lama? \ ‏לָמָה?‏

wife/woman \ isha \ ‏אִשָּׁה‏

wind \ ru'ach \ ‏רוּחַ‏

window \ chalon \ ‏חַלּוֹן‏

wine \ yayin \ ‏יַיִן‏

winter \ choref \ ‏חֹרֶף‏

with \ im \ ‏עִם‏

with pleasure! \ bekeif! \ ‏בְּכֵיף!‏

worry \ do'eg \ ‏דּוֹאֵג‏

write \ kotev \ ‏כּוֹתֵב‏

yard \ chatzer \ ‏חָצֵר‏

year \ shana \ ‏שָׁנָה‏

yellow \ tzahov \ ‏צָהֹב‏

yes \ ken \ ‏כֵּן‏

yeshiva style \ yeshivati \ ‏יְשִׁיבָתִי‏

yesterday \ etmol \ ‏אֶתְמוֹל‏

you (f,pl) \ aten \ ‏אַתֶּן‏

you (f) \ at \ ‏אַתְּ‏

you (m,pl) \ atem \ ‏אַתֶּם‏

you (m) \ ata \ ‏אַתָּה‏

you want to leave a message? \ rotzeh lehash'ir hoda'a? \ ‏רוֹצֶה לְהַשְׁאִיר הוֹדָעָה?‏

you're welcome \ bivakasha \ ‏בְּבַקָּשָׁה‏

young \ tza'ir \ ‏צָעִיר‏

your (f,pl) \ shelchen \ ‏שֶׁלָּכֶן‏

your (f) \ shelach \ ‏שֶׁלָּךְ‏

your (m,pl) \ shelchem \ ‏שֶׁלָּכֶם‏

your (m) \ shelcha \ ‏שֶׁלְּךָ‏

youth pass \ kartis no'ar \ ‏כַּרְטִיס נֹעַר‏

אַבָּא \ aba \ father

אָבִיב \ aviv \ spring

אֲבָנִים \ avanim \ stones

אַבְרֵךְ \ avrech \ kollel guy

אֱגוֹזִים \ egozim \ nuts

אֲגַם \ agam \ lake

אַגָס \ agas \ pear

אָדֹם \ adom \ red

אַוָז \ avaz \ goose

אוֹטוֹ, רֶכֶב \ oto, rechev \ car

אוֹטוֹבּוּס \ otobus \ bus

אוֹי וַאֲבוֹי \ Oy-va-voy! \ Oh no!

אֲוִיר \ avir \ air

אוּלַי \ ulai \ maybe

אוֹמֵר \ omer \ say

אוֹפֶה \ ofeh \ bake

אוֹפַנוֹעַ \ ofano'a \ motorcycle

אוֹפַנַּיִם \ ofanayim \ bicycle

אֹרֶז \ orez \ rice

אוֹתוֹ דָבָר \ oto davar \ same thing

אֹזֶן \ ozen \ ear

אָח \ ach \ brother

אָחוֹת \ achot \ sister

אַחְיָן \ achyan \ nephew

אַחְיָנִית \ achyanit \ niece

אַחֲרוֹן אַחֲרוֹן חָבִיב \ achron achron chaviv \ last but not least

אַחֲרֵי \ achrei \ after

אַחֲרֵי הַצָהֳרַיִם \ achrei hatzaharayim \ afternoon

אִטְרִיוֹת \ itri'ot \ noodles

אֵיזֶה מְטֹרָף! \ eizeh metoraf! \ what a jerk!

אֵיזֶה צֶבַע זֶה? \ eizeh tzeva zeh? \ what color is this?

אֵיזֶה ... \ eizeh... \ what a...

אֵיזֶה? \ eizeh? \ which?

אֵיךְ אַתָּה מַרְגִיש (אַתְ מַרְגִישָׁה)? \ eich ata margish (at margisha)? \ how are you feeling?

אֵיךְ מַגִיעִים לְ...? \ eich magi'im le...? \ how do i get to?

אֵיךְ? \ eich? \ how?

אֵין הֶבְדֵל \ ein hevdel \ no difference

אֵין לִי זְמַן \ ein li zman \ i don't have any time

אֵין לִי כֹּחַ \ ein li ko'ach \ i don't have any energy

אֵין לִי \ ein li \ i don't have

אֵין מַצָב \ ein matzav \ no way jose

אֵין סָפֵק \ ein safek \ no doubt

אֵיפֹה? \ eifo? \ where?

אַל תַּפְרִיעַ לִי \ al tafri'a li \ i don't bother me

אִמָּא \ ima \ mother

אֲנַחְנוּ \ anachnu \ we

אֲנִי \ Ani \ I

אֲנִי אוֹהֵב (אוֹהֶבֶת) לֶאֱכוֹל... \ Ani ohev (ohevet) le'echol... \ I like to eat......

אֲנִי אוֹהֵב (אוֹהֶבֶת)... \ Ani ohev (ohevet)... \ I like

אֲנִי בְּסֵדֶר \ Ani beseder \ I'm fine

אֲנִי חוֹשֵׁב (חוֹשֶׁבֶת) שֶׁלֹא \ Ani choshev (choshevet) shelo \ I don't think so

אֲנִי יוֹדֵעַ (יוֹדַעַת) \ Ani yode'a (yoda'at) \ I know

אֲנִי כְּבָר יוֹדֵעַ (יוֹדַעַת) \ Ani kvar yode'a (yoda'at) \ I know already

אֲנִי כּוֹעֵס (כּוֹעֶסֶת) \ Ani ko'es (ko'eset) \ I am angry

אֲנִי לֹא אוֹהֵב (אוֹהֶבֶת)... \ Ani lo ohev (ohevet)... \ I don't like

אֲנִי לֹא זוֹכֵר (זוֹכֶרֶת) \ Ani lo zocher (zocheret) \ I don't remember

אֲנִי לֹא יוֹדֵעַ (יוֹדַעַת) \ Ani lo yode'a (yoda'at) \ I don't know

אֲנִי לֹא מֵבִין (מְבִינָה) \ Ani lo mevin (mevina) \ I don't understand

אֲנִי לֹא מַרְגִּישׁ טוֹב (מַרְגִּישָׁה טוֹבָה) \ Ani lo margish tov (margisha tova) \ I don't feel well

אֲנִי לֹא מְרֻצֶּה (מְרֻצָּה) \ Ani lo merutzeh (merutza) \ I am not pleased

אֲנִי לוֹבֵשׁ (לוֹבֶשֶׁת) אֶת הַ_____ שֶׁלִּי \ Ani lovesh (loveshet) et ha_____ sheli \ I wear my _____

אֲנִי לוֹמֵד (לוֹמֶדֶת) עִבְרִית \ Ani lomed (lomedet) Ivrit \ I'm learning Hebrew

אֲנִי מְבֻלְבָּל (מְבֻלְבֶּלֶת) \ Ani mivulbal (mivulbelet) \ I am confused

אֲנִי מֻדְאָג (מֻדְאֶגֶת) \ Ani mud'ag (mud'eget) \ I am worried

אֲנִי מְפַחֵד (מְפַחֶדֶת) \ Ani mefached (mefachedet) \ I am scared

אֲנִי מַרְוִיחַ הַרְבֵּה כֶּסֶף (מַרְוִיחָה) \ Ani marvi'ach (marvicha) harbeh kesef \ I make a lot of money

אֲנִי מְרֻצֶּה (מְרֻצָּה) \ Ani merutzeh (merutza) \ I am pleased

אֲנִי מִתְבַּיֵּשׁ (מִתְבַּיֶּשֶׁת) \ Ani mitbayesh (mitbayeshet) \ I am embarrassed

אֲנִי מִתְחָרֵט (מִתְחָרֶטֶת) \ Ani mitcharet (mitcharetet) \ I regret

אֲנִי מִתְרַגֵּשׁ (מִתְרַגֶּשֶׁת) \ Ani metragesh (mitrageshet) \ I am excited

אֲנִי עוֹבֵד בְּמִשְׂרָד גָּדוֹל (עוֹבֶדֶת) \ Ani oved (ovedet) bemisrad gadol \ I work in a big office

אֲנִי עָיֵף (עֲיֵפָה) \ Ani ayeif (ayeifa) \ I am tired

אֲנִי עָצוּב (עֲצוּבָה) \ Ani atzuv (atzuva) \ I am sad

אֲנִי צָמֵא (צְמֵאָה) \ Ani tzameh (tzme'a) \ I am thirsty

אֲנִי רוֹצֶה לֶאֱכֹל בּוּרֶקָס (רוֹצָה) \ Ani rotzeh (rotza) le'echol burekas \ I want to eat borekas

אֲנִי רוֹצֶה לְדַבֵּר עִבְרִית (רוֹצָה) \ Ani rotzeh (rotza) ledaber Ivrit \ I want to speak Hebrew

אֲנִי רוֹצֶה לִקְנוֹת (רוֹצָה) \ Ani rotzeh (rotza) liknot \ I want to buy

אֲנִי רָעֵב (רְעֵבָה) \ Ani ra'ev (re'eva) \ I am hungry

אֲנִי שׂוֹנֵא (שׂוֹנֵאת) \ Ani soneh (sona't)... \ I hate

אֲנִי שָׂמֵחַ (שְׂמֵחָה) \ Ani same'ach (smecha) \ I am happy

אֲנִי \ Ani ... \ I am a...

אֲנִי... \ Ani... \ I'm...

אֶס אֶם אֶס \ sms \ text message

אַף \ af \ nose

אָפֹר \ afor \ gray

אֲפַרְסֵק \ afarsek \ peach

אֶפְשָׁר לְדַבֵּר עִם יוֹסִי? \ Efshar ledaber im Yossi? \ Can I speak with Yossi?

אֶפְשָׁר לָלֶכֶת לְשָׁם בָּרֶגֶל? \ Efshar lalechet lesham baregel? \ Can I get there by foot?

אֶצְבַּע \ etzba \ finger

אֲרוּחַת בֹּקֶר \ aruchat boker \ breakfast

אֲרוּחַת עֶרֶב \ aruchat erev \ dinner

אֲרוּחַת צָהֳרַיִם \ aruchat tzaharayim \ lunch

אָרֹךְ \ aroch \ long

אָרוֹן \ aron \ closet

אֲרוֹן סְפָרִים \ aron sfarim \ book shelf

אַרְיֵה \ aryeh \ lion

אַרְנָק \ arnak \ wallet

אֶרֶץ \ eretz \ land

אִשָּׁה \ isha \ wife/woman

אֶשְׁכּוֹלִית \ eshkolit \ grapefruit

אַתְּ \ at \ you (f)

אַתָּה \ ata \ you (m)

אַתָּה מַצְבִּיעַ? \ ata matzbi'a? \ Are you voting?

אַתֶּם \ atem \ you (m,pl)

אֶתְמוֹל \ etmol \ yesterday

אַתֶּן \ aten \ you (f,pl)

אֲתָר \ atar \ website

בְּ \ be... \ in

בָּא \ ba \ come

בֶּאֱמֶת \ be'emet \ truthfully

בֶּאֱמֶת?(!) \ be'emet?(!) \ indeed?(!)

בַּבֹּקֶר \ baboker \ in the morning

בְּבַקָשָׁה \ bevakasha \ please

בְּבַקָשָׁה \ bivakasha \ you're welcome

בְּדִיּוּק \ bediyuk \ exactly

בָּהִיר \ bahir \ light (adj)

בָּהִיר \ bahir \ sunny

בְּהַצְלָחָה! \ behatzlacha! \ good luck!

בּוֹא לְפֹה \ bo lepo \ come here

בְּוַדַאי \ bevadai \ certainly

בּוֹיְדֶעם \ boydem \ attic

בּוֹכֶה \ bocheh \ cry

בּוֹץ \ botz \ mud

בּוֹרֵחַ \ bore'ach \ run away

בַּחוּץ \ bachutz \ out

בְּחִירוֹת \ bechirot \ election

בַּחֲלוֹמוֹת \ bachalomot \ in your dreams

בֶּטֶן \ beten \ belly

בַּיי! \ Bai! \ Bye!

בֵּייגְלָךְ \ beigalach \ pretzels

בֵּין \ bein \ between

בֵּיצִים \ beitzim \ eggs

בִּירָה \ bira \ beer

בְּיִשְׂרָאֵל לֹא יוֹרֵד גֶּשֶׁם בַּקַּיִץ \ BeYisra'el lo yored geshem bakayitz \ In Israel it doesn't rain in the summer

בַּיִת \ bayit \ house/home

בֵּית כְּנֶסֶת \ beit keneset \ synagogue

בֵּית סֵפֶר \ beit sefer \ school

בְּכֵיף! \ bekeif! \ with pleasure!

בַּלַּיְלָה \ balaila \ at night

בְּמָה אַתָּה עוֹבֵד (אֵת עוֹבֶדֶת)? \ Bema ata oved (at ovedet)? \ what kinda work do you do?

בֵּן \ ben \ son

בֶּן דּוֹד \ ben dod \ cousin

בִּנְיָן \ binyan \ building

בָּנָנָה \ banana \ banana

בְּסֵדֶר \ beseder \ fine

בְּסֵדֶר \ Beseder \ Okay

בַּעַל \ baal \ husband

בָּעֶרֶב \ ba'erev \ In the evening

בַּצַּד \ batzad \ on the side

בָּצָל \ batzal \ onion

בֹּקֶר טוֹב! \ Boker tov! \ Good morning!

בַּרְוָז \ barvaz \ duck

בָּרוּךְ הַשֵּׁם, מְצֻיָּן \ Baruch Hashem, metzuyan \ Thank G-d, great

בֶּרֶז \ berez \ faucet

בֶּרֶךְ \ berech \ knee

בָּרַמְזוֹר \ baramzor \ at the traffic light

בָּרָק \ barak \ lightning

בִּשְׁבִיל \ bishvil \ for

בַּשּׁוּק יֵשׁ הַרְבֵּה סוּגֵי פֵּרוֹת \ Bashuk yesh harbeh sugei peirot \ In the shuk there are many kinds of fruits

בָּשָׂר \ basar \ meat

בַּת \ bat \ daughter

בְּתוֹךְ \ betoch \ inside

בָּתִּים \ batim \ houses

גַּב \ gav \ back

גָּבוֹהַ \ gavoha \ tall

גַּבּוֹת \ gabot \ eyebrows

גְּבִינָה \ gvina \ cheese

גֶּבֶר \ gever \ man

גַּג \ gag \ roof

גָּדוֹל \ gadol \ big

גָּדַלְנוּ בְּיַחַד \ Gadalnu biyachad \ We grew up together

גָּדֵר \ gader \ gate

גּוֹמֵר \ gomer \ end

גּוּף \ guf \ body

גֶּזַע \ geza \ tree trunk

גֶּזֶר \ gezer \ carrot

גִּיס \ gis \ brother-in-law

גִּיסָה \ gisa \ sister-in-law

גַּם \ gam \ also

גָּמָל \ gamal \ camel

גִּנָּה \ gina \ garden

גַּרְבַּיִם \ garbayim \ socks

גַּרְעִינִים \ gar'inim \ sunflower seeds

גֶּשֶׁר \ gesher \ bridge

ד"ש \ dash \ regards

דֹּב \ dov \ bear

דָּג \ dag \ fish

דּוֹאֵג \ do'eg \ worry

דּוּבְדְּבָן \ duvdevan \ cherry

דּוֹד \ dod \ uncle

דּוֹדָה \ doda \ aunt

דְּלַעַת \ dla'at \ squash

דֶּלֶת \ delet \ door

דֶּלֶת אֲחוֹרִית \ delet achorit \ back door

דֶּלֶת קִדְמִית \ delet kidmit \ front door

דָּם \ dam \ blood

דַּף הַבַּיִת \ daf habayit \ homepage

דַּק \ dak \ thin

דַּקָּה \ daka \ minute

דָּרוֹם \ darom \ south

דֶּרֶךְ אַגַב \ derech agav \ by the way

דֶּשֶׁא \ desheh \ grass

הַבֵּן שֶׁלִּי אוֹהֵב אֶת גַּן הַחַיּוֹת \ Haben sheli ohev et gan hachayot \ My son loves the zoo

הַדּוּבְדְּבָן שֶׁבַּקְצֶפֶת \ haduvdevan shebakatzefet \ the cherry on the cream

הַדֶּשֶׁא יָרֹק \ Hadesheh yarok \ The grass is green

הוּא \ hu \ he

הוּא אֹכֵל הַרְבֵּה \ Hu ochel harbeh \ He eats a lot of...

הוּא לֹא יָכוֹל לְדַבֵּר עַכְשָׁו \ Hu lo yachol ledaber achshav \ He can't speak now

הוּא עָקַף אוֹתִי! \ Hu akaf oti! \ He cut me off!

הוֹדוּ \ hodu \ turkey

הוֹרִים \ horim \ parents

הִיא \ hi \ she

הִיא אוֹהֶבֶת לֶאֱכוֹל... \ Hi ohevet le'echo... \ She loves to eat...

הַיּוֹם \ hayom \ today

הֲכִי טוֹב! \ Hachi tov! \ The best!

הַכֹּל \ hakol \ all

הָלוֹ! \ Allo! \ Hello! (only used when answering phone)

הָלוֹךְ וְחָזוֹר \ haloch vachazor \ round trip

הֵם \ hem \ they (m)

הַמִּשְׁפָּחָה מַגִּיעָה לְשַׁבָּת \ Hamishpacha magi'a leShabat \ The family is coming for Shabbos

הֵן \ hen \ they (f)

הַצֶּבַע שֶׁאֲנִי הֲכִי אוֹהֵב הוּא כָּחֹל \ Hatzeva she'ani hachi ohev hu kachol \ My favorite color is blue

הַקּוֹל שֶׁלִּי לֹא מַשְׁפִּיעַ \ Hakol sheli lo mashpi'a \ My vote doesn't make a difference

הַקַּשׁ שֶׁשָּׁבַר אֶת גַּב הַגָּמָל \ hakash sheshavar et gav hagamal \ the straw that broke the camel's back

הַר \ har \ mountain

הַרְבֵּה \ harbeh \ a lot

הַרְבֵּה זְמַן \ harbeh zman \ a long time

הַרְבֵּה שָׁנִים \ harbeh shanim \ many years

הַשָּׁנָה הַבָּאָה \ hashana haba'a \ next year

הַשָּׁנָה הַזֹּאת \ hashana hazot \ this year

הַשָּׁנָה שֶׁעָבְרָה \ hashana she'avra \ last year

הַשָּׁעָה שְׁתַּיִם \ hasha'a shtayim \ two o'clock

וְ... \ ve... \ and

וַי וַי! \ Wai wai! \ Whoa!

וָרֹד \ varod \ pink

זֶה \ zeh \ this

זֶה בֶּאֱמֶת קַל? \ Zeh be'emet kal? \ Is it actually easy?

זֶה בָּרִיא לֶאֱכֹל יְרָקוֹת \ Zeh bari le'echol yerakot \ It's healthy to eat vegetables

זֶה דָּחוּף? \ Zeh dachuf? \ Is the mater urgent?

זֶה כָּחֹל \ Zeh kachol \ This is blue

זֶה לֹא בְּסֵדֶר \ Zeh lo beseder \ That's not cool/That's not okay

זֶה לֹא הָעֵסֶק שֶׁלְּךָ (שֶׁלָּךְ) \ Zeh lo ha'esek shelcha (shelach) \ It's not your business

זֶה רָחוֹק מִכָּאן? \ Zeh rachok mikan? \ Is it far from here?

זֶה רַק דִּבּוּרִים \ Zeh rak diburim \ It's only talk

זֶה... \ Zeh... \ It's...

זָהָב \ zahav \ gold

זֶהוּ זֶה \ Zehu zeh \ That's it

זוֹחֵל \ zochel \ crawl

זוֹכֵר \ zocher \ remember

זוֹל \ zol \ cheap

זוֹרֵק \ zorek \ throw

זַיִת \ zayit \ olive

זְמַן \ zman \ time

זָקָן \ zakan \ beard

זְרוֹעַ \ zro'a \ arm

חֲבָל עַל הַזְּמַן \ chaval al hazman \ totally awesome (lit a waste of time)

חֲבֵר כְּנֶסֶת \ chaver keneset \ member of parliament

חֲבֵרִים \ chaverim \ friends

חֲגוֹרָה \ chagora \ belt

חֶדֶר \ cheder \ room

חֲדַר שֵׁנָה \ chadar sheina \ bedroom

חֹדֶשׁ \ chodesh \ month

חָדָשׁ \ chadash \ new

חֹדֶשׁ טוֹב! \ Chodesh tov! \ Good month!

חוֹל \ chol \ sand

חוּם \ chum \ brown

חוּמוּס \ chumus \ hummus

חוֹסֵךְ \ chosech \ save

חוֹף \ chof \ beach

חוֹשֵׁב \ choshev \ think

חוֹתֵךְ \ chotech \ cut

חוֹתֵן, שְׁוֶר \ choten, shver \ father-in-law

חָזָק \ chazak \ strong

חֲטִיפִים \ chatifim \ junk-food

חַי \ chai \ live

חַכֵּה רֶגַע \ Chakeh rega \ Wait a second

חָלָב \ chalav \ milk

חַלּוֹן \ chalon \ window

חֲלִיפָה \ chalifa \ suit

חֻלְצָה \ chultza \ shirt

חַלָּשׁ \ chalash \ weak

חַם \ cham \ hot

חֶמְאָה \ chema \ butter

חֲמוֹר \ chamor \ donkey

חָמוֹת \ chamot \ mother-in-law

חֲנֻיּוֹת \ chanuyot \ stores

חֲצִי שָׁעָה \ chatzi sha'a \ a half of an hour

חָצֵר \ chatzer \ yard

חֹרֶף \ choref \ winter

חָשׁוּב \ chashuv \ important

חֲתוּלָה \ chatula \ cat

חָתָן \ chatan \ son-in-law

טוֹב \ tov \ good

טֶכְנוֹלוֹגְיָה \ technologiya \ technology

טֶלֶפוֹן נַיָּד, פֵּלֶאפוֹן \ telefon nayad, pelefon \ cell phone

טָעִים \ ta'im \ tasty

יַאללָה בַּיי \ yala bai \ goodbye

יָבֵשׁ \ yavesh \ dry

יָד \ yad \ hand

יוֹדֵעַ \ yode'a \ know

יוֹם \ yom \ day

יוֹם חֲמִישִׁי \ Yom Chamishi \ Thursday

יוֹם טוֹב! \ Yom tov! \ Good day!

יוֹם רִאשׁוֹן \ Yom Rishon \ Sunday

יוֹם רְבִיעִי \ Yom Revi'i \ Wednesday

יוֹם שְׁלִישִׁי \ Yom Shlishi \ Tuesday

יוֹם שֵׁנִי \ Yom Sheni \ Monday

יוֹם שִׁשִּׁי \ Yom Shishi \ Friday

יוֹצֵא דֹּפֶן \ yotzeh dofen \ unusual

יוֹרֵד גֶּשֶׁם \ Yored geshem \ It's raining

יוֹרֵד שֶׁלֶג \ Yored sheleg \ It's snowing

יוֹשֵׁב \ yoshev \ sit

יַיִן \ yayin \ wine

יֶלֶד \ yeled \ boy

יַלְדָּה \ yalda \ girl

יְלָדִים \ yeladim \ children

יָם \ yam \ sea

יָמִים יַגִּידוּ \ yamim yagidu \ time will tell

יָמִינָה \ Yamina \ Take a right

יָפֶה מְאֹד \ yafeh me'od \ very nice

יָפֶה/נָעִים \ yafe/na'im \ nice

יָקָר \ yakar \ expensive

יָרֵחַ \ yare'ach \ moon

יָרֵךְ \ yarech \ thigh

יָרֹק \ yarok \ green

יֵשׁ לִי כֹּחַ \ Yesh li ko'ach \ I have energy

יֵשׁ לִי \ Yesh li \ I have

יְשִׁיבָתִי \ yeshivati \ yeshiva style

יָשָׁן \ yashan \ old

יָשָׁר יָשָׁר עַד הַסּוֹף \ yashar yashar ad hasof \ go all the way to the end

יָשָׁר \ yashar \ straight ahead

כְּבִישׁ \ kvish \ road

כְּבִישׁ מָהִיר \ kvish mahir \ highway

כֶּבֶשׂ \ keves \ sheep

כֵּהֶה \ keheh \ dark

כּוֹאֵב לִי הַיָּד \ ko'ev li hayad \ my hand hurts

כּוֹבַע \ kova \ hat

כּוֹכָבִים \ kochavim \ stars

כּוֹכָבִית \ kochavit \ star key (telephone)

כּוֹתֵב \ kotev \ write

כָּחֹל \ kachol \ blue

כִּיּוֹר \ kiyor \ sink

כִּיס \ kis \ pocket

כִּירַיִם \ kirayim \ stove

כָּכָה זֶה הוֹלֵךְ \ kacha zeh holech \ that's how it goes

כָּכָה כָּכָה \ kacha kacha \ so so

כָּל-יוֹם \ kol yom \ everyday

כֶּלֶב \ kelev \ dog

כַּלָּה \ kala \ daughter-in-law

כְּלוּם \ klum \ nothin' at all

כְּלֵי עֲבוֹדָה \ klei avoda \ tools

כַּמָּה שָׁנִים \ kama shanim \ a couple of years

כַּמָּה? \ kama? \ how much?

כְּמוֹ שֶׁצָּרִיךְ \ kimo shetzarich \ the way it should be

כֵּן \ ken \ yes

כְּנֶסֶת \ knesset \ parliament

כִּסֵּא \ kiseh \ chair

כֶּסֶף \ kesef \ money

כֶּסֶף \ kesef \ silver

כִּפָּה \ kipa \ skullcap

כִּפָּה סְרוּגָה \ kipa sruga \ knit skullcap

כַּפִּית \ kapit \ spoon

כְּפָפוֹת \ k'fafot \ gloves

כְּרוּב \ kruv \ cabbage

כַּרְטִיס נוֹעַר \ kartis no'ar \ youth pass

כַּרְטִיסִיָּה \ kartisiya \ bus pass

כַּרְטִיסִיָּה רְגִילָה \ kartisiya regila \ adult pass

כָּרִיךְ\סֶנְדְּוִיץ' \ karich/sendvitsh \ sandwich

כָּרִית \ karit \ pillow

כָּתֹם \ katom \ orange (color)

כָּתֵף \ katef \ shoulder

לְ... \ le... \ to

לֹא \ lo \ no

לֹא טוֹב \ lo tov \ not good

לֹא יֵאָמֵן \ lo ye'uman \ unbelievable

לֹא יִתָּכֵן \ lo yitachen \ can't be

לֹא כָּכָה \ lo kacha \ not like that

לֹא לְהַגְזִים! \ lo lehagzim \ don't exaggerate

לֹא מְשַׁנֶּה \ lo meshaneh \ it doesn't make a difference/never mind

לֹא תּוֹדָה \ lo toda \ no thanks

לְאַט \ le'at \ slow

לֵב \ lev \ heart

לָבָן \ lavan \ white

לִגְלֹשׁ \ liglosh \ to surf

לְהַצְבִּיעַ \ lehatzbi'a \ to vote

לְהַרְוִיחַ \ leharvi'ach \ to profit

לְהִתְרָאוֹת! \ lehitra'ot! \ see you later!

לֹוֶה \ loveh \ borrow

לוֹקֵחַ \ loke'ach \ take

לַח \ lach \ humid

לֶחִי \ lechi \ cheek

לֶחֶם \ lechem \ bread

לַחְמָנִיָּה \ lachmaniya \ roll

לַיְלָה טוֹב! \ laila tov! \ good night!

לִימוֹן \ limon \ lemon

לֵךְ מִכָּאן \ lech mikan \ go away

לָמָה? \ lama? \ why?

לְמַטָּה \ lemata \ down

לְמִי אַתָּה מַצְבִּיעַ? \ lemi ata matzbi'a? \ Who are you voting for?

לְמַעְלָה \ lema'ala \ up

לִפְנֵי \ lifnei \ before

לִפְנֵי הַצָּהֳרַיִם \ lifnei hatzaharayim \ before noon

לִפְנֵי שְׁבוּעַיִם \ lifnei shvu'ayim \ two weeks ago

לָשׁוֹן \ lashon \ tongue

מְאַבֵּד \ me'abed \ lose

מְאַוְרֵר \ me'avrer \ fan

מֵאֲחוֹרֵי \ me'achorei \ behind

מְאֻחָר \ me'uchar \ late

מֵאֵיפֹה אַתָּה (אַתְּ)? \ Me'eifo ata (at)? \ Where're you from?

מֵאָלֶף עַד תָּיו \ me'alef ad tav \ from A to Z

מַאֲמִין \ ma'amin \ believe

מְאַרְגֵּן \ me'argen \ organize

מַבּוּל \ mabul \ flood

מֵבִיא \ mevi \ bring

מְבַקֵר \ mevaker \ visit

מְבַקֵש \ mevakesh \ request

מְבָרֵך \ mevarech \ bless

מְבַשֵל \ mevashel \ cook

מַגֶבֶת \ magevet \ towel

מַגָפַיִם \ magafayim \ boots

מְגֵרָה \ megera \ drawer

מַגָש \ magash \ tray

מַדְהִים \ madhim \ awesome

מַדְעָן (מַדְעָנִית) \ mad'an (ma'adanit) \ scientist

מַדְרֵגוֹת \ madregot \ stairs

מִדְרָכָה \ midracha \ sidewalk

מָה אכְפַת לִי? \ Ma ichpat li? \ What do I care?

מָה אַתָה אוֹמֵר (אַתְ אוֹמֶרֶת)?! \ Mah ata omer (at omeret)?! \ What are you talkin' about?! (this expression means : Really?!)

מָה אַתָה עוֹשֶׂה (אַתְ עוֹשָׂה) בַחַיִים? \ Ma ata oseh (at osa) bachayim? \ What do you do for a living?

מָה הוּא רוֹצֶה לֶאֱכוֹל? \ Ma hu rotzeh le'echol? \ What does he want to eat?

מָה הָעִנְיָנִים? \ Ma ha'inyanim? \ How are things?

מָה חָדָש? \ Ma chadash? \ What's new?

מָה מֶזֶג הָאֲוִיר? \ Eich mezeg ha'avir? \ How's the weather?

מָה נִשְׁמָע? \ Ma nishma? \ What's up?

מָה פִּתְאוֹם?! \ Ma pitom?! \ What in the world?! (lit what suddenly)

מָה קוֹרֶה? \ Ma koreh? \ What's happening?

מָה קָרָה? \ Ma kara? \ What happened? מַה שְׁלוֹמְך (שְׁלוֹמֵך) \ Ma shlomcha (shlomech)? \ How are you?

מָה? \ Ma? \ What?

מְהֻדָק \ mehudak \ tight

מְהַנְדֵּס (מְהַנְדֶּסֶת) \ mehandes (mehandeset) \ engineer

מַהֵר \ maher \ fast

מוֹדֶה \ modeh \ thank

מוּזָר \ muzar \ strange

מוֹכֵר \ mocher \ sell

מוּל \ mul \ opposite

מוֹצֵא \ motzeh \ find

מוֹרֶה (מוֹרָה) \ moreh (mora) \ teacher

מֶזֶג הָאֲוִיר הוּא...... \ Mezeg ha'avir hu...... \ The weather is...

מַזְכִּיר \ mazkir \ remind

מַזְכִּיר (מַזְכִּירָה) \ mazkir (mazkira) \ secretary

מַזְלֵג \ mazleg \ fork

מִזְרָח \ mizrach \ east

מַחְבֶּרֶת \ machberet \ notebook

מַחֲבַת \ machvat \ pan

מְחַיֵיך \ mechayech \ smile

מְחַכֶּה \ mechakeh \ wait

מַחְלִיף \ machlif \ exchange

מְחַפֵּש \ mechapes \ search

מָחָר \ machar \ tomorrow

מָחֳרָתַיִם \ machratayim \ the day after tomorrow

מַחְשֵׁב \ machshev \ computer

מַחְשֵׁב נַיָד \ machshev nayad \ laptop

מְחֻתָּנִים \ mechutanim \ in-laws

מִטְבָּח \ mitbach \ kitchen

מִטָה \ mita \ bed

מָטוֹס \ matos \ airplane

מְטַיֵל \ metayel \ take a stroll

מִי זֶה? \ Mi zeh? \ Who is this?

מִי? \ Mi? \ Who?

מֵייל \ meil \ email

מִים \ mayim \ water

מִיץ \ mitz \ juice

מַכִּיר \ makir \ recognize

מִכְנָסַיִם \ michnasayim \ pants

מְכַסֶּה \ mechaseh \ cover

מָלֵא \ maleh \ full

מְלַוֶּה \ melaveh \ escort

מַלְוֶה \ malveh \ lend

מֶלוֹן \ melon \ melon

מֶלַח \ melach \ salt

מִלְחִיָּה \ milchiya \ salt shaker

מְלֻכְלָךְ \ meluchlach \ dirty

מְלָפְפוֹן \ melafefon \ cucumber

מֶמְשָׁלָה \ memshala \ government

מְנַהֵל (מְנַהֶלֶת) \ menahel (minahelet) \ CEO

מִנְהָרָה \ minhara \ tunnel

מָנוֹעַ חִפּוּשׂ \ mano'a chipus \ search engine

מְנַסֶּה \ menaseh \ try

מְנַקֶּה \ menakeh \ clean (verb)

מִסָּבִיב \ misaviv \ around

מָסָךְ \ masach \ screen

מַסְפִּיק \ maspik \ enough

מְסַפֵּר \ mesaper \ tell over (ie a story)

מִסְתַּכֵּל \ mistakel \ look

מַעֲבַר חֲצִיָּה \ ma'avar chatzaya \ crosswalk

מְעִיל \ me'il \ coat

מַעְיָן \ ma'ayan \ natural spring

מֵעַל \ me'al \ over

מְעַנְיֵן \ me'anyen \ interesting

מְעֻנָּן \ me'unan \ cloudy

מַעֲרָב \ ma'arav \ west

מַפִּיּוֹן \ mapiyon \ napkin

מַפָּל \ mapal \ waterfall

מַפְרִיעַ \ mafri'a \ disturb

מַפְתְּחוֹת \ maftechot \ keys

מֵצַח \ metzach \ forehead

מְצֻיָּן \ metzuyan \ great

מְצַיֵּר \ metzayer \ sketch

מַצֶּקֶת \ matzeket \ ladle

מְקַבֵּל \ mekabel \ receive

מֻקְדָּם \ mukdam \ early

מְקַוֶּה \ mekaveh \ hope

מִקְלֶדֶת \ mikledet \ keyboard

מַרְאֶה \ mar'eh \ show

מַרְגִּישׁ \ margish \ feel

מֵרִיחַ \ meri'ach \ smell

מִרְפֶּסֶת \ mirpeset \ balcony

מָרָק \ marak \ soup

מַרְשֶׁה \ marsheh \ allow

מַרְתֵּף \ martef \ basement

מַשָּׂאִית \ masa'it \ truck

מַשֶּׁהוּ מַשֶּׁהוּ! \ Masheu masheu! \ It's very very good!

מְשׂוֹחֵחַ \ mesoche'ach \ schmooze

מְשַׂחֵק \ mesachek \ play

מִשְׂחָקִים \ mischakim \ toys

מִשְׁטָרָה \ mishtara \ police

מַשְׂכִּיר \ maskir \ rent out

מַשְׂכֹּרֶת \ maskoret \ salary

מְשַׁלֵּם \ meshalem \ pay

מִשְׁמֵשׁ \ mishmesh \ apricot

מְשַׁנֶּה \ meshaneh \ change

מַשְׁקֶה חָרִיף \ mashke charif \ liquor

מִשְׁקָפַיִם \ mishkafayim \ glasses

מִתְגָּאֶה \ mitga'eh \ take pride

מִתַּחַת \ mitachat \ under

מָתַי? \ Matai? \ When?

מִתְפַּלֵּל \ mitpalel \ pray

מְתַקֵן \ metaken \ fix

נְבָטִים \ nevatim \ sprouts

נֶהָג חָדָש \ nehag chadash \ new driver

נִהְיֶה בְּקֶשֶׁר \ Nihyeh bekesher \ We'll be in touch

נָהָר \ nahar \ river

נוֹסֵע \ nose'a \ travel

נוֹרְמָלִי \ normali \ normal

נוֹתֵן \ noten \ give

נָחָשׁ \ nachash \ snake

נִין \ nin \ great-grandchild

נְיָר \ niyar \ paper

נֶכֶד \ neched \ grandchild

נָכוֹן \ nachon \ correct

נָמוּךְ \ namuch \ low

נָמֵר \ namer \ tiger

נְסִיעָה טוֹבָה! \ Nesiya tova! \ Have a good trip!

נָעִים \ na'im \ pleasant

נֶעֱלַבְתִּי \ Ne'elavti \ I am insulted

נַעֲלַיִם \ na'alayim \ shoes

נָפַל לוֹ בֹּרֶג \ Nafal lo boreg \ He's got a screw loose

נָקִי \ naki \ clean (adj)

נִרְאֶה לִי שֶׁכֵּן \ Nireh li sheken \ It seems so

נִשְׁבַּר לִי \ Nishbar li \ I've had it

נָשִׂיא \ nasi \ president

נְשָׁמָה \ neshama \ sweetheart

נָתִיב \ netiv \ lane

סַבָּא \ saba \ grandfather

סַבָּא רַבָּה \ saba raba \ great grandfather

סַבְתָּא \ savta \ grandmother

סַבְתָּא רַבָּה \ savta raba \ great grandmother

סָגוֹל \ segol \ purple

סָגוּר \ sagur \ closed

סְגוֹר אֶת הַחַלּוֹן \ S'gor et hachalon \ Close the window

סוֹגֵר \ soger \ close (verb)

סוּלָמִית \ sulamit \ pound key (telephone)

סוּס \ sus \ horse

סוֹעֵר בַּחוּץ \ So'er bachutz \ It's stormy outside

סוֹף שָׁבוּעַ \ sof shavu'a \ weekend

סוֹפֵר \ sofer \ count

סְטוּדֶנְט (סְטוּדֶנְטִית) \ student (studentit) \ student

סִיר \ sir \ pot

סַכִּין \ sakin \ knife

סֻכָּר \ sukar \ sugar

סָלוֹן \ salon \ living room

סָלָט \ salat \ salad

סְלִיחָה \ slicha \ excuse me

סֶלֶרִי \ seleri \ celery

סֹלֶת וּשְׁמֶנָה \ salta veshamna \ cream of the crop

סִסְמָא \ sisma \ password

סְעָרָה \ se'ara \ storm

סַפָּה \ sapa \ couch

סַפְסָל \ safsal \ bench

סְפָרִים \ sfarim \ books

סְתָיו \ stav \ fall

עָבֶה \ aveh \ thick

עַגְבָנִיָּה \ agvaniya \ tomato

עוּגָה \ uga \ cake

עוּגִיָּה \ ugiya \ cookie

עַד \ ad \ until

עֲדַיִן לֹא \ adayin lo \ not yet

עוֹד הַפַּעַם \ od hapa'am \ again

עוֹזֵר \ ozer \ help (verb)

עוֹנֶה \ oneh \ answer

עוֹף \ ohf \ chicken	פָּנִים \ panim \ face
עוֹרֵךְ (עוֹרֶכֶת) דִּין \ orech (orechet) din \ lawyer	פַּס הָאֵטָה \ pas he'ata \ speed bump
עוֹשֶׂה \ oseh \ do	פְּצָצָה \ p'tzatza \ excellent
עֵט \ et \ pen	פָּרָה \ para \ cow
עַיִן \ ayin \ eye	פְּרָחִים \ prachim \ flowers
עִיתּוֹנַאי (עִיתּוֹנָאִית) \ itonai (itona'it) \ journalist	פָּתוּחַ \ patu'ach \ open (adj)
עַכְבָּר \ achbar \ mouse	צְבִי \ tzvi \ deer
עַכְשָׁו \ achshav \ now	צָהֹב \ tzahov \ yellow
עַכְשָׁו אֲנִי לוֹמֵד (לוֹמֶדֶת) לְדַבֵּר \ Achshav ani lomed (lomedet) ledaber \ I'm now learning to speak	צָהֳרַיִם \ tzaharayim \ noon
	צָהֳרַיִם טוֹבִים! \ Tzaharayim tovim! \ Good afternoon!
עַל \ al \ on	צַוָּאר \ tzavar \ neck
עַל הַפָּנִים \ al hapanim \ horrible	צוֹבֵעַ \ tzove'a \ color
עַל יָד \ al yad \ next to	צוֹחֵק \ tzochek \ laugh
עִם \ im \ with	צוֹעֵק \ tzo'ek \ scream
עֲנָבִים \ anavim \ grapes	צַלַּחַת \ tzalachat \ plate
עָנִי \ ani \ poor	צִלְצוּל \ tziltzul \ ring
עֲנִיבָה \ aniva \ tie	צְמָחִים \ tzmachim \ vegetation
עֲנָנִים \ ananim \ clouds	צֹמֶת \ tzomet \ intersection
עֲנָפִים \ anafim \ branches	צְנוֹן \ tznon \ radish
עִפָּרוֹן \ iparon \ pencil	צָעִיף \ tza'if \ scarf
עֵץ \ etz \ tree	צָעִיר \ tza'ir \ young
עֶצֶם \ etzem \ bone	צָפוֹן \ tsafon \ north
עֶרֶב טוֹב! \ Erev tov! \ Good evening!	צִפּוֹר \ tzipor \ bird
מְעוּרְפָּל \ arafel \ foggy	צְפַרְדֵּעַ \ tzfardei'a \ frog
עָשִׁיר \ ashir \ rich	צִפֹּרֶן \ tziporen \ nail
עִיתּוֹן \ iton \ newspaper	קַבָּלָה \ kabala \ receipt
פֶּה \ pe \ mouth	קוֹאָלִיצְיָה \ ko'alitzi'a \ coalition
פֹּה/כָּאן \ po/kan \ here	קוֹלָה \ kola \ cola
פּוֹתֵחַ \ pote'ach \ open (verb)	קוֹף \ kof \ monkey
פַּח \ pach \ garbage can	קוֹפֵץ \ kofetz \ jump
פִּיל \ pil \ elephant	קוֹרֵא \ koreh \ call
פָלָאפֶל \ falafel \ falafel	קָטָן \ katan \ small
פִּלְפֵּל \ pilpel \ pepper	קַיִץ \ kayitz \ summer

קִיר \ kir \ wall

קַל \ kal \ easy/easy-shmeezy

קַל מְאֹד \ kal me'od \ very easy

קוּמְקוּם \ kumkum \ kettle

קָפֶה \ kafeh \ coffee

קָצָר \ katzar \ short

קְצָת \ ketzat \ a little

קְצָת זְמָן \ ketzat zman \ a little time

קַר \ kar \ cold

קְרָא לְרוֹפֵא \ K'ra lerofeh \ Call a doctor

קָרוֹב \ karov \ close (adj)

קָרִיר \ karir \ cool

קְרֵקֶרִים \ krekerim \ crackers

קָשֶׁה \ kasheh \ difficult

קָשֶׁה \ kasheh \ hard

קִשּׁוּר \ kishur \ link

קֶשֶׁת \ keshet \ rainbow

רֹאשׁ \ rosh \ head

רֹאשׁ הַמֶּמְשָׁלָה \ rosh hamemshala \ prime minister

רֹאשׁ הָעִיר \ rosh ha'ir \ mayor

רַב \ rav \ rabbi

רַב קַו \ rav kav \ bus card

רֶבַע שָׁעָה \ reva sha'a \ a quarter of an hour

רֶגֶל \ regel \ foot

רֶגַע \ rega \ moment

רִהוּט \ rihut \ furniture

רוֹאֶה \ ro'eh \ see

רוּחַ \ ru'ach \ wind

רוֹחֵץ \ rochetz \ wash

רוֹפֵא (רוֹפְאָה) \ rofeh (rof'a) \ doctor

רוֹפֵא (רוֹפְאַת) שִׁנַּיִם \ rofeh (rof'at) shinayim \ dentist

רוֹצֶה לְהַשְׁאִיר הוֹדָעָה? \ Rotzeh lehash'ir hoda'a? \ You want to leave a message?

רוֹקֵד \ roked \ dance

רְחוֹב \ rechov \ street

רָחוֹק \ rachok \ far

רָטוּב \ ratuv \ wet

רֵיק \ reik \ empty

רַךְ \ rach \ soft

רִמּוֹן \ rimon \ pomegranate

רַמְזוֹר \ ramzor \ traffic light

רַע \ ra \ bad

רְעִידַת אֲדָמָה \ re'idat adama \ earthquake

רַעַם \ ra'am \ thunder

רָפוּי \ rafui \ loose

רָץ \ ratz \ run

רִצְפָּה \ ritzpa \ floor

רַק \ rak \ only

רִשְׁיוֹן נְהִיגָה \ risheyon nehiga \ driver's license

שֵׁב (שְׁבִי) \ Shev (Sh'vi) \ Have a seat

שָׁבוּעַ \ shavu'a \ week

שָׁבוּעַ טוֹב! \ Shavu'a tov! \ Good week!

שָׁבוּר \ shavur \ broken

שַׁבָּת \ Shabbat \ Saturday

שָׂדֶה \ sadeh \ field

שׁוֹאֵל \ sho'el \ ask

שׂוֹחֶה \ socheh \ swim

שׁוֹכֵב \ shochev \ lie down

שׁוֹכֵחַ \ shoche'ach \ forget

שׂוֹכֵר \ socher \ rent

שׁוֹלֵחַ \ shole'ach \ send

שׁוּם \ shum \ garlic

שׁוֹמֵעַ \ shome'a \ hear

שׁוֹמֵר \ shomer \ guard

שׁוּעָל \ shu'al \ fox

שׁוֹפֵךְ \ shofech \ pour

שׁוֹתֶה \ shoteh \ drink
שׁוֹתֵק \ shotek \ be silent
שֶׁזִיף \ shezif \ plum
שָׁחוֹר \ shachor \ black
שְׁטוּיוֹת \ shtuyot \ nonsense
שַׁיִשׁ \ shayesh \ counter
שָׁכַחְתִּי \ Shachachti \ I forgot
שֶׁלָּהּ \ shela \ hers
שֶׁלָּהֶם \ shelhem \ their (m)
שֶׁלָּהֶן \ shelhen \ their (f)
שֶׁלּוֹ \ shelo \ his
שָׁלוֹם! \ Shalom! \ Hello/Goodbye!
שֻׁלְחָן \ shulchan \ table
שֶׁלִּי \ sheli \ mine
שֶׁלָּךְ \ shelach \ your (f)
שֶׁלְּךָ \ shelcha \ your (m)
שֶׁלָּכֶם \ shelchem \ your (m,pl)
שֶׁלָּכֶן \ shelchen \ your (f,pl)
שָׁלֵם \ shalem \ complete
שֶׁלָּנוּ \ shelanu \ our
לִפְנֵי יוֹמַיִם \ lifnei yomayim \ two days ago
שָׁם \ sham \ there
שְׂמֹאלָה \ Smola \ Take a left
שְׁמֹר לִי, אֶשְׁמֹר לְךָ \ Shmor li, eshmor licha \ I'll scratch your back you scratch mine
שְׂמִיכָה \ smicha \ blanket
שָׁמַיִם \ shamayim \ sky
שִׂמְלָה \ simla \ dress
שֶׁמֶשׁ \ shemesh \ sun
שָׁנָה \ shana \ year
שְׁנִיָּה \ shniya \ second
שִׁנַּיִם \ shinayim \ teeth
שָׁעָה \ sha'a \ hour
שְׁעוֹן יָד \ sha'on yad \ watch

שְׁעוּעִית \ sha'u'it \ beans
שֵׂעָר \ se'ar \ hair
שָׂפָם \ safam \ moustache
שְׂפָתַיִם \ sfatayim \ lips
שְׁקֵדִים \ shkedim \ almonds
שֶׁקֶט! \ Sheket! \ Be quiet!
שֶׁקַע \ sheka \ electric outlet
שַׂר \ sar \ minister
שָׁר \ shar \ sing
שֵׁרוּתִים \ sherutim \ bathroom
שָׁרָשִׁים \ sharashim \ roots
שְׁתִיָּה חַמָּה \ shtiya chama \ hot drink
שְׁתִיָּה קָרָה \ shtiya kara \ cold drink
תָּא הַקּוֹלִי \ ta hakoli \ voice mail
תְּאוּרָה \ te'ura \ lights
תְּאֵנָה \ te'ena \ fig
תַּגִּיד שׁוּב \ Tagid Shuv \ Say it again
תְּדַבֵּר (תְּדַבְּרִי) קְצָת יוֹתֵר לְאַט \ Tedaber (Tedabri) ktzat yoter le'at \ Speak a little slower
תֵּה \ tei \ tea
תּוֹדָה רַבָּה \ toda raba \ thank you very much
תּוֹדָה \ toda \ thank you
תּוֹכְנָה \ tochna \ program
תּוּת \ tut \ berry
תַּחֲזִית \ tachazit \ forecast
תַּחֲנָה מֶרְכָּזִית \ tachana merkazit \ central bus station
תַּחֲנַת אוֹטוֹבּוּס \ tachanat otobus \ bus stop
תַּחְתּוֹנִים \ tachtonim \ underwear
תִּיק \ tik \ purse
תָּמָר \ tamar \ date
תֶּן לִי כּוֹס... \ Ten li kos... \ Give me a glass of
תַּנּוּר \ tanur \ oven
תְּנַסֶּה מְאֻחָר יוֹתֵר \ Tenaseh me'uchar yoter

\ Try later

תִּסְתַּכֵּל (תִּסְתַּכְּלִי) \ Tistakel (Tistakli) \ Have a look

תַּעֲזֹב אוֹתִי \ Ta'azov oti \ Leave me alone

תַּעֲמוּלָה \ ta'aluma \ propaganda

תַּפּוּז \ tapuz \ orange (fruit)

תַּפּוּחַ \ tapu'ach \ apple

תַּפּוּחַ אֲדָמָה \ tapu'ach adama \ potato

תִּקְרָה \ tikra \ ceiling

תַּקְשִׁיב (תַּקְשִׁיבִי) \ Takshiv (Takshivi) \ Listen up

תַּרְגִּישׁ (תַּרְגִּישִׁי) \ Targish (Targishi) בַּבַּיִת \ babayit \ Make yourself at home

תִּתְקַשֵּׁר אֵלַי מָחָר \ Titkasher elai machar \ Call me tomorrow

Go to **www.EasyShmeezy.com** to download mp3 lessons that walk you through the book every step of the way. In no time you'll be speakin' like a real sabra.

In memory of Jerry Ganz and Menashe "Nash" Kestenbaum. Two great men who are missed every day by their families and friends.

Shmuli and Deena Ganz & family

Do You Want to Take Your Language
Learning to a New Level?

FluencyFreedom.com

Finally, Learn the Language of Your Dreams!